FASTING

IN RAMADAAN

as observed by the Prophet (ﷺ)

by
Shaikh Saleem al-Hilaalee
and
Shaikh 'Alee Hasan 'Alee 'Abdul-Hameed

Translated by Aboo Talhah Daawood ibn Ronald Burbank

Second Edition

ISBN 1 898649 07 3

British Library Cataloguing in Publication Data.
A catalogue record for this book is available from the British Library.

First Edition, 1994.
Second Edition, 1995.

© Copyright 1995 by Al-Hidaayah Publishing and Distribution

Printed by All Trade Printers, Birmingham, U.K.

Typeset by Al-Hidaayah Publishing & Distribution

Cover illustration by Ishtiaq Khan

Published by   Al-Hidaayah Publishing & Distribution
                   P.O. Box 3332
                   Birmingham
                   United Kingdom
                   B10 9AW

                   Tel: 0121 753 1889
                   Fax: 0121 753 2422

Contents

Publisher's Note

All praise is for Allaah, Lord of the worlds, prayers and peace be upon Muhammad, his family, his companions and all those who follow in his footsteps until the Last Day.

Alhamdulillaah, before you is the English translation of the Arabic book *Sifah Sawm An-Nabee.* It will *inshaallaah* serve as a beneficial book for all those who do not give precedence to anyone above Allaah and His Messenger (ﷺ).

Books of this nature are long overdue in the English language, as English speaking Muslims have been deprived of authentic books based on the Glorious Qur'aan and the Pure *Sunnah* upon the understanding of the Pious Predecessors. Instead they have had to rely on poorly re-searched books full of unauthentic *ahaadeeth,* and innovated practices. We hope that this book helps the reader to perfect his fast so that it may be acceptable to Allaah and of benefit to us on the Day of Resurrection.

We would like to thank all the brothers and sisters who helped in the publication of this book, particularly Aboo Talhah.

Finally, if you find errors in the book please inform us so that we may correct them in future editions.

All praise is for Allaah who made this task possible for us.

Al-Hidaayah Publishing and Distribution.

Note: All references refer to the Arabic books unless otherwise stated.

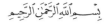

Introduction

Verily, all praises are for Allaah. We praise Him, we seek His aid and ask for His forgiveness, and we seek Allaah's refuge from the evils of ourselves and from our evil actions. Whomsoever Allaah guides then there is none to misguide him, and whomsoever Allaah misguides then there is none to guide him. I testify that none has the right to be worshipped but Allaah alone, having no partner, and I testify that Muhammad (ﷺ) is His slave and His Messenger. To proceed:

O brother, may Allaah unite us upon love of Him and upon following the *Sunnah* of His Messenger (ﷺ). The status of fasting and its place in Islaam will become clear to us and also the great reward awaiting the one who fasts seeking the Face of Allaah,[1] and how that reward increases or decreases depending on its closeness to the *Sunnah* of the Messenger (ﷺ), as was indicated by the best of the children of Aadam(ﷺ) who said: *"Perhaps a person fasting will receive nothing from his fasting except hunger and thirst."*[2]

Therefore, we must know the characteristics of the Prophet's (ﷺ) fast; its obligatory duties, its manners and related supplications - and then put that into practice.

Since it is difficult for most people to acquire detailed knowledge of this, we decided to compile a book which would, as far as possible, gather everything related to how the Prophet (ﷺ) fasted in Ramadaan and so be useful to all the Muslims, the Believers who do not give anything precedence over Allaah and His Messenger.

---

1. **Publisher's note:** This expression means seeking to see Allaah on the Day of Judgement. See Sooratul-Qiyaamah (75):22-3 and Sooratul-Insaan(76):9.

2. Reported by Ibn Maajah (1/539), ad-Daarimee (2/211), Ahmad (2/441 and 373) and al-Baihaqee (4/270) by way of Sa'eed al-Maqbaree from Aboo Hurairah, and its chain of narration is *saheeh*.

After examining the *Aayaat* concerning fasting and the authentic *ahaadeeth* we find that fasting is of two types: obligatory fasting and optional fasting.

So, seeking the aid of Allaah, we began writing about the obligatory fast since a Muslim cannot draw near to Allaah with anything better than those things which He has made obligatory as occurs in the *hadeeth* reported by al-Bukhaaree.[3]

We decided to order the book and its chapters in accordance with the stages through which the obligation of fasting passed, then in accordance with how the fast is practically observed.

So whatever you find within it to be correct and good, then it is from Allaah, the Most High and any mistakes that you find in it are from us and from *Shaytaan* and we disassociate ourselves from that whether in our lives or after our deaths, and we ask Allaah to grant us success in doing what is correct - *indeed He is the One Who hears and responds.*

Written by two students of knowledge of the *Sharee'ah*:

Saleem al-Hilaalee and
'Alee Hasan 'Alee 'Abdul-Hameed.
25th Ramadaan 1403H.

---

3. **Publisher's note:** Full text of *hadeeth*: On the authority of Aboo Hurairah, who said that the Messenger of Allaah said: Allaah, the Mighty and Majestic, said:

"Whoever shows enmity to someone devoted to Me, I shall be at war with him. My servant draws not near to Me with anything more loved by Me than the obligatory duties, and My servant continues to draw near to Me with optional works so that I shall love him. When I love him I am his hearing with which he hears, his seeing with which he sees, his hand with which he strikes and his foot with which he walks. Were he to ask (something) of Me, I would surely give it to him, and were he to ask Me for refuge, I would surely grant him it. I do not hesitate about anything as much as I hesitate about (seizing) the soul of My faithful servant; he hates death and I hate hurting him."

Chapter 1

Virtues of Fasting

Clear and decisive verses in the Noble Book of Allaah encourage fasting as a means of seeking nearness to Allaah the Mighty and Majestic, and explain its virtues, such as the Saying of Allaah, the Most High:

$$\text{إِنَّ ٱلْمُسْلِمِينَ وَٱلْمُسْلِمَـٰتِ وَٱلْمُؤْمِنِينَ وَٱلْمُؤْمِنَـٰتِ وَٱلْقَـٰنِتِينَ}$$
$$\text{وَٱلْقَـٰنِتَـٰتِ وَٱلصَّـٰدِقِينَ وَٱلصَّـٰدِقَـٰتِ وَٱلصَّـٰبِرِينَ وَٱلصَّـٰبِرَٰتِ وَٱلْخَـٰشِعِينَ}$$
$$\text{وَٱلْخَـٰشِعَـٰتِ وَٱلْمُتَصَدِّقِينَ وَٱلْمُتَصَدِّقَـٰتِ وَٱلصَّـٰٓئِمِينَ وَٱلصَّـٰٓئِمَـٰتِ}$$
$$\text{وَٱلْحَـٰفِظِينَ فُرُوجَهُمْ وَٱلْحَـٰفِظَـٰتِ وَٱلذَّٰكِرِينَ ٱللَّهَ كَثِيرًا}$$
$$\text{وَٱلذَّٰكِرَٰتِ أَعَدَّ ٱللَّهُ لَهُم مَّغْفِرَةً وَأَجْرًا عَظِيمًا ﴿٣٥﴾}$$

"Verily, the Muslim men and women, the believing men and women, the men and women who are obedient (to Allaah), the men and women who are truthful (in their speech and deeds), the men and the women who are patient, the men and the women who are humble (before their Lord), the men and the women who give charity, *the men and the women who fast,* **the men and the women who guard their chastity (from illegal sexual acts) and the men and the women who remember Allaah much. Allaah has prepared for them forgiveness and a great reward (i.e. Paradise)."**[1]

---

1. Sooratul-Ahzaab (33):35

1

Allaah the Majestic says:

$$\textcircled{\scriptsize ١٨٤} \ وَأَن تَصُومُوا۟ خَيْرٌ لَّكُمْ إِن كُنتُمْ تَعْلَمُونَ$$

"...and fast, it is better for you, if only you knew.'[2]

Allaah's Messenger (ﷺ) explained in the established *Sunnah* that fasting is protection from desires, a shield from the Fire, and that Allaah has particularised one of the gates of Paradise for it. It will lead the soul away from its desires, and prevent it from those things which it has come to find attractive, so that it becomes tranquil. This great reward and huge blessing is explained beautifully and fully in the following authentic *ahaadeeth*.

• Fasting is a shield

Allaah's Messenger (ﷺ) ordered the one who has strong desires and the need for marriage, but is unable to marry, to fast. He (ﷺ) declared it as a means of cutting off the desires, since it reduces the vigour of the limbs of the body, calms them and bridles them. It is established that it has a great effect in preserving the limbs and organs, we therefore find that he(ﷺ) said: *"O youths, whoever amongst you is able to marry then let him do so, since it restrains the eyes and protects the private parts, and he who is unable, then let him fast because it is a shield for him."*[3]

Allaah's Messenger (ﷺ) also informed us of how Paradise is surrounded by hardships and that the Fire is surrounded by desires. So when you know, O Muslim, that fasting subdues the desires and reduces their severity, and that it is these which lead to the Fire, then you will see how fasting comes between a fasting person and the Fire. There are clear *ahaadeeth* stating that fasting is a protection from the Fire, and a shield by which the servant may protect himself from it.

---

2. Sooratul-Baqarah (2):184

3. Reported by al-Bukhaaree and Muslim from Ibn Mas'ood.

2

He (ﷺ) said: *"There is not a servant who fasts a day in the way of Allaah, except that Allaah removes his face from the Fire by the distance of seventy years because of that."*[4]

He (ﷺ) said: *"Fasting is a shield with which a servant protects himself from the Fire."*[5]

He (ﷺ) said: *"Whoever fasts a day in the way of Allaah, Allaah will place between him and the Fire a trench like that between the heavens and the earth.'*[6]

Some scholars hold that these *ahaadeeth* refer to the excellence of fasting whilst fighting *Jihaad* in the way of Allaah. However what is apparent is that every fast that is done sincerely, seeking the Face of Allaah, the Most High, in the way that was explained by Allaah's Messenger (ﷺ), is *in the way of Allaah.*

• Fasting causes one to enter Paradise

Obedient servant: may Allaah grant that you are obedient to Him, and may He aid you, you have come to know that fasting distances a person from the Fire and it therefore causes him to draw closer to the midst of Paradise. Aboo Umaamah, *radiyallaahu 'anhu,* said: I said: *"O Messenger of Allaah tell me of an action by which I may enter Paradise."* He said: *"Take to Fasting, there is nothing like it."*[7]

---

4. Reported by al-Bukhaaree (6/35) and Muslim (no. 1153) from Aboo Sa'eed al-Khudree and the wording is that of Muslim.

5. Reported by Ahmad (3/241, 296) from Jaabir, and Ahmad (4/22) from Uthmaan Ibn Abil-'Aas, and the *hadeeth* is *saheeh*

6. Reported by at-Tirmidhee (no. 1624) from the *hadeeth* of Aboo Umaamah, and its chain of narration contains some weakness - al-Waleed ibn Jameel is *sadooq* (truthful, with fair memory) but he makes mistakes. However he is supported, since at-Tabaraanee reports in *al-Kabeer* (8/260, 273, 280) by way of two chains from al-Qaasim from Aboo Umaamah. Its like is also reported from Aboo Dardaa' by at-Tabaraanee in *as-Sagheer* (1/273) - and it contains weakness. So the *hadeeth* is *saheeh.*

7. Reported by an-Nasaa'ee (4/165), Ibn Hibbaan (p.232 of *al-Mawaarid*), and al-Haakim (1/421), its chain of narration is *saheeh.*

• The people who fast are rewarded with immense reward

A great reward awaits the person who fasts, he experiences joy twice - once in this world and once in the hereafter, and even the smell coming from his mouth is better with Allaah than the smell of musk.

Aboo Hurairah, *radiyallaahu 'anhu*, said: Allaah's Messenger (ﷺ) said: "*Allaah said that all of the actions of the son of Aadam are for him except for fasting, for it is for Me and I will recompense it. Fasting is a shield, and when it is the day when one of you fasts, then let him not speak indecently or argue, and if anyone abuses or seeks to fight him then let him say, 'I am fasting.' By Him in whose Hand is the soul of Muhammad the smell coming from the mouth of the fasting person is better with Allaah then the smell of musk. For the fasting person there are two times of joy; when he breaks his fast he is happy and when he meets his Lord he is happy due to his fasting.'*[8]

In a narration reported by al-Bukhaaree there occurs: "*...He abandons his food and drink and desires because of Me, fasting is for Me and I will grant recompense for it, and a good deed is rewarded ten times over.*"

In a narration of Muslim there occurs: "*Every action of the son of Aadam is given manifold reward, each good deed receiving ten times its like, up to seven hundred times. Allaah the Most High said, 'Except for fasting, for it is for Me and I will give recompense for it, he leaves off his desires and his food for Me.' For the fasting person there are two times of joy; a time of joy when he breaks his fast and a time of joy when he meets his Lord, and the smell coming from the mouth of the fasting person is better with Allaah than the smell of musk.*"

---

8. Reported by al-Bukhaaree (4/118) and Muslim (no.1151), the wording is that of al-Bukhaaree.

• Fasting and the Qur'aan intercede for a person

He (ﷺ) said: *"Fasting and the Qur'aan intercede for the servant on the Day of Resurrection. Fasting will say: O My Lord I prevented him from food and desires so accept my intercession for him, and the Qur'aan will say: I prevented him from sleep at night, so accept my intercession for him, so their intercession will be accepted."* [9]

• Fasting is an expiation for various sins

Amongst those virtues which are particular to fasting is that Allaah has made it an expiation for:

(a) Shaving the head whilst in a state of *ihraam* for one who does that due to some illness

(b) One who is unable to carry out the obligatory sacrifice

(c) Accidentally killing one of a people with whom you have a treaty

(d) Hunting game whilst in a state of *ihraam*

(e) Violating an oath

(f) *Dhihaar* [10]

All this is explained in the following *Aayaat:*

---

9. Reported by Ahmad (no.6626), al-Haakim (1/554), Aboo Nu'aim (8/161) and others from 'Abdullaah ibn 'Amr, and its chain of narration is *hasan.*

Note: As for this *hadeeth* and its like which refer to the embodiment of actions, then it is obligatory to have full and certain faith in them, without distorting the meaning or misinterpreting it, since this is the way of the Pious Predecessors (*as-Salafus-Saalih*) and it is without a doubt safer, based upon knowledge and wiser, not to mention the fact that it is one of the most important conditions of *Eemaan.* Allaah the Most High says:

"...who believe in the *Ghayb* (unseen) and offer the prayers perfectly and spend out of what we have provided for them. "
Sooratul-Baqarah (2):3

10. **Publisher's note:** This is the saying of the husband to his wife: You are to me like the back of my mother (i.e. unlawful for me).

Allaah the Most High Says:

وَأَتِمُّوا۟ الْحَجَّ وَالْعُمْرَةَ لِلَّهِ ۚ فَإِنْ أُحْصِرْتُمْ فَمَا اسْتَيْسَرَ مِنَ الْهَدْىِ ۖ وَلَا تَحْلِقُوا۟ رُءُوسَكُمْ حَتَّىٰ

بَلَغَ الْهَدْىُ مَحِلَّهُ ۚ فَمَن كَانَ مِنكُم مَّرِيضًا أَوْ بِهِۦٓ أَذًى مِّن رَّأْسِهِۦ فَفِدْيَةٌ مِّن صِيَامٍ

أَوْ صَدَقَةٍ أَوْ نُسُكٍ ۚ فَإِذَآ أَمِنتُمْ فَمَن تَمَتَّعَ بِالْعُمْرَةِ إِلَى الْحَجِّ فَمَا اسْتَيْسَرَ مِنَ الْهَدْىِ ۚ فَمَن

لَّمْ يَجِدْ فَصِيَامُ ثَلَٰثَةِ أَيَّامٍ فِى الْحَجِّ وَسَبْعَةٍ إِذَا رَجَعْتُمْ ۗ تِلْكَ عَشَرَةٌ كَامِلَةٌ ۗ ذَٰلِكَ لِمَن لَّمْ

يَكُنْ أَهْلُهُۥ حَاضِرِى الْمَسْجِدِ الْحَرَامِ ۚ وَاتَّقُوا۟ اللَّهَ وَاعْلَمُوٓا۟ أَنَّ اللَّهَ شَدِيدُ الْعِقَابِ ﴿١٩٦﴾

"And perform properly the *Hajj* **and** *'Umrah* **for Allaah. But if you are prevented (from completing them), sacrifice an animal such as you can afford, and do not shave your heads until the animal reaches the place of sacrifice. And whosoever of you is ill or has an ailment in his scalp (necessitating shaving), he must pay a ransom of either fasting (three days) or giving charity (to feed six poor persons) or offering a sacrifice (of one sheep). Then if you are in safety and whoever performs** *'Umrah* **in the months of** *Hajj,* **before (perform-ing) the** *Hajj,* **he must slaughter an animal such as he can afford, but if he cannot afford it,** *he should fast three days during the Hajj and seven days after his return (to his home), making ten days in all.* **This is for him whose family is not present at al-Masjidul-Haram (i.e. non-resident of Makkah). And fear Allaah much and know that Allaah is severe in punishment."**[11]

Allaah the Majestic says:

وَإِن كَانَ مِن قَوْمٍ بَيْنَكُمْ وَبَيْنَهُم مِّيثَٰقٌ فَدِيَةٌ مُّسَلَّمَةٌ إِلَىٰٓ

أَهْلِهِۦ وَتَحْرِيرُ رَقَبَةٍ مُّؤْمِنَةٍ ۖ فَمَن لَّمْ يَجِدْ فَصِيَامُ شَهْرَيْنِ

مُتَتَابِعَيْنِ تَوْبَةً مِّنَ اللَّهِ ۗ وَكَانَ اللَّهُ عَلِيمًا حَكِيمًا ﴿٩٢﴾

---

11. Sooratul-Baqarah (2):196

"...and if he (the one who was killed) belonged to a people with whom you have a treaty of mutual alliance, compensation (of blood-money) must be paid to his family, and a believing slave must be freed. And whosoever finds this (the penance of freeing a slave) beyond his means, *he must fast for two consecutive months in order to seek repentance from Allaah.* And Allaah is Ever All-Knowing All-Wise."[12]

The All-Hearing and All-Knowing said:

لَا يُؤَاخِذُكُمُ اللَّهُ بِاللَّغْوِ فِىٓ أَيْمَٰنِكُمْ وَلَٰكِن يُؤَاخِذُكُم بِمَا عَقَّدتُّمُ الْأَيْمَٰنَ فَكَفَّٰرَتُهُۥٓ إِطْعَامُ عَشَرَةِ مَسَٰكِينَ مِنْ أَوْسَطِ مَا تُطْعِمُونَ أَهْلِيكُمْ أَوْ كِسْوَتُهُمْ أَوْ تَحْرِيرُ رَقَبَةٍ فَمَن لَّمْ يَجِدْ فَصِيَامُ ثَلَٰثَةِ أَيَّامٍ ذَٰلِكَ كَفَّٰرَةُ أَيْمَٰنِكُمْ إِذَا حَلَفْتُمْ وَاحْفَظُوٓا۟ أَيْمَٰنَكُمْ كَذَٰلِكَ يُبَيِّنُ اللَّهُ لَكُمْ ءَايَٰتِهِۦ لَعَلَّكُمْ تَشْكُرُونَ ﴿٨٩﴾

"Allaah will not punish you for what is unintentional in your oaths, but He will punish you for your deliberate oaths; for its expiation feed ten poor persons, on a scale of the average of that with which you feed your own families, or clothe them, or manumit a slave.*But whosoever cannot afford (that), then he should fast for three days. That is the expiation for the oaths when you have sworn.* And protect your oaths (i.e. do not swear much). Thus Allaah makes clear to you His *Aayaat* that you may be grateful."[13]

The Mighty and the Wise says:

---

12. Sooratun-Nisaa' (4):92

13. Sooratul-Maa'idah (5):89

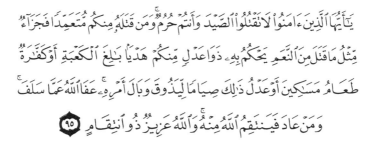

"O you who believe! Kill not game while you are in a state of *ihraam*, and whosoever of you kills it intentionally, the penalty is an offering, brought to the Ka'bah, of an eatable animal equivalent to the one he killed, as adjudged by two just men among you, or for expiation, he should feed poor persons, *or its equivalent in fasting*, that he may taste the heaviness (punishment) of his deed. Allaah has forgiven what is past, but whosoever commits it again, Allaah will take retribution from him. And Allaah is All-Mighty, All-Able of Retribution."[14]

And the One who knows everything and is fully aware of even the most hidden affairs says:

وَٱلَّذِينَ يُظَٰهِرُونَ مِن نِّسَآئِهِمْ ثُمَّ يَعُودُونَ لِمَا قَالُوا فَتَحْرِيرُ رَقَبَةٍ مِّن قَبْلِ أَن يَتَمَآسَّا ۚ ذَٰلِكُمْ تُوعَظُونَ بِهِۦ ۚ وَٱللَّهُ بِمَا تَعْمَلُونَ خَبِيرٌ ۝ فَمَن لَّمْ يَجِدْ فَصِيَامُ شَهْرَيْنِ مُتَتَابِعَيْنِ مِن قَبْلِ أَن يَتَمَآسَّا ۖ فَمَن لَّمْ يَسْتَطِعْ فَإِطْعَامُ سِتِّينَ مِسْكِينًا ۚ ذَٰلِكَ لِتُؤْمِنُوا بِٱللَّهِ وَرَسُولِهِۦ ۚ وَتِلْكَ حُدُودُ ٱللَّهِ ۗ وَلِلْكَٰفِرِينَ عَذَابٌ أَلِيمٌ ۝

"And those who make unlawful for themselves (their own wives by *dhihaar*) and wish to free themselves from what they uttered, (the penalty) in that case (is) the freeing of a slave before they touch each

---

14. Sooratul-Maa'idah (5):95

other. That is an admonition to you (so that you may not return to such an ill thing). And Allaah is All-Aware of what you do. *And he who finds not (the money for freeing a slave) must fast two successive months before they both touch each other.* And for him who is unable to do so, he should feed sixty of the poor (who beg). That is in order that you may have perfect faith in Allaah and His Messenger. These are the limits set by Allaah. And for the disbelievers, there is a painful torment."[15]

Likewise fasting, (prayer) and charity wipe away the evils caused for a man through his wealth, family and neighbour: From Hudhaifah ibn al-Yamaan, *radiyallaahu 'anhu*, who said: He (ﷺ) said: *"The evils caused for a man through his family, wealth and neighbour are expiated by prayer, fasting and charity."*[16]

• *Ar-Rayyaan* is for those who fast

From Sahl ibn Sa'd, *radiyallaahu 'anhu*, that the Prophet (ﷺ) said: *"Indeed there is a gate of Paradise called ar-Rayyaan. On the day of Resurrection those who fast will enter through it; no one enters it except for them, and when they have entered, it is closed so that no one enters it, [so when the last of them enters it, it is closed, and whoever enters it drinks, and whoever drinks never becomes thirsty.]"*[17]

---

15. Sooratul-Mujaadilah (58):3-4

16. Reported by al-Bukhaaree (2/7) and Muslim (no. 144).

17. Reported by al-Bukhaaree (4/95) and Muslim (no. 1152) and the final addition is reported by Ibn Khuzaimah in his *Saheeh* (no. 1903).

9

Chapter 2

Virtues of Ramadaan

Ramadaan is a month of goodness and blessings and Allaah has distinguished it with many virtues:

• It is the month of the Qur'aan

Allaah the Mighty and Majestic sent down His Noble Book as a guide for the people and a cure for the Believers, guiding to what is best, and explaining the correct path, and it was revealed on *Lailatul-Qadr* during the blessed month of Ramadaan. The Owner of the *'Arsh* (throne), The Most Noble says:

شَهْرُ رَمَضَانَ ٱلَّذِىٓ أُنزِلَ فِيهِ ٱلْقُرْءَانُ هُدًى لِّلنَّاسِ وَبَيِّنَـٰتٍ مِّنَ ٱلْهُدَىٰ وَٱلْفُرْقَانِ فَمَن شَهِدَ مِنكُمُ ٱلشَّهْرَ فَلْيَصُمْهُ

"The month of Ramadaan in which was revealed the Qur'aan, a guidance for mankind and clear proofs for the guidance and the Criterion (between right and wrong). So whoever of you sights (the crescent on the first night of) the month (of Ramadaan), he must fast that month." [1]

And know, O brother, may Allah send blessings upon you, that (in the above verse) concerning the description of Ramadaan, and (information) that the

---

1. Sooratul-Baqarah (2):185

10

Qur'aan was sent down in it, is followed by what comes after the letter *faa* which in the Arabic language indicates purpose and reason:

$$\text{فَمَن شَهِدَ مِنكُمُ ٱلشَّهْرَ فَلْيَصُمْهُ}$$

"*So whoever of you sights (the cresent of the first night of) the month (of Ramadaan), he must fast that month.*"

This indicates that Ramadaan is the month of fasting because the Qur'aan was revealed during it.

• In it the devils are chained, the gates of Hell-Fire are locked and the gates of Paradise are opened

So evil is lessened in this blessed month since the evil *jinn*[2] are bound with chains, shackles and bonds. Thus, they are unable to corrupt the people as they do at other times, since the Muslims are occupied with fasting which subdues desires, and with reciting the Qur'aan and with other acts of worship which refine and purify the souls. The Lord of Honour and Power says:

$$\text{كُتِبَ عَلَيْكُمُ ٱلصِّيَامُ كَمَا كُتِبَ عَلَى ٱلَّذِينَ مِن قَبْلِكُمْ لَعَلَّكُمْ تَتَّقُونَ ﴿١٨٣﴾}$$

"*Fasting is prescribed for you as it was prescribed for those before you, that you may attain* taqwa.*"*[3]

Therefore the gates of Hell are locked and the gates of Paradise are opened since righteous actions are many and good words are plentiful. He (ﷺ) said:

---

2. **Publisher's note:** *Jinn:* A creation of Allaah, made from smokeless fire, among whom are some who are obedient to Allaah and others who are not.

3. Sooratul-Baqarah (2):183

11

"When Ramadaan comes the gates of paradise[4] are opened, the gates of Hell-Fire are locked and the devils are chained."[5]

All of this is done during the first night of the blessed month, as he (ﷺ) said: *"When it is the first night of the month of Ramadaan the evil devils are chained. The gates of the Fire are locked - not a single gate is opened, and the gates of Paradise are opened - not a single gate is locked, and a caller calls out: O seeker of good come forward, and O seeker of evil withhold, and there are many whom Allaah frees from the Fire - and that is every night."[6]*

• *Lailatul-Qadr* (The Night of Decree)

You have seen, O believing servant, how Allaah the Majestic has chosen Ramadaan, since the Noble Qur'aan was sent down in it, and from this point other things may be inferred:

(a) The most excellent of the days before Allaah is in the month in which He sent down the Qur'aan, so this must be particularised with extra actions. This is supported by what is reported about seeking *Lailatul-Qadr* and seeking to perform extra actions in it, and this will come, if Allaah wills, in the chapter concerning *Lailatul-Qadr*.

(b) That the blessing which has come to the Muslims necessitates an increase in action out of gratefulness to Allaah, and this is supported by the saying of the Creator after mention of the completion of the blessing of the month of Fasting:

---

4. One wording of Muslim is: *'The gates of mercy are opened'*.

5. Reported by al-Bukhaaree (4/97) and Muslim (no. 1079).

6. Reported by at-Tirmidhee (no. 682), Ibn Maajah (no. 1642), and Ibn Khuzaimah (3/188). This chain of narration is *hasan*.

"(He wants that you) must complete the same number (of days), and that you must glorify Allaah for having guided you so that you may be grateful to Him."[7]

His, the Blessed and the Most High's, Saying after mention of the completion of the blessing of *Hajj*:

فَإِذَا قَضَيْتُم مَّنَاسِكَكُمْ فَاذْكُرُوا اللَّهَ كَذِكْرِكُمْ ءَابَآءَكُمْ أَوْ أَشَدَّ ذِكْرًا

"So when you have accomplished your rites (of *Hajj*) remember Allaah as you remember your father or with a far greater remembrance."[8]

---

7. Sooratul-Baqarah (2):185

8. Sooratul-Baqarah (2):200

Chapter 3

The Obligation to Fast in Ramadaan

• Whoever does extra of his own accord then it is better for him

Due to the virtues which have been mentioned, Allaah made it obligatory upon the Muslims to fast during the month of Ramadaan. However, since it is extremely difficult to wean the soul away from its desires and to prevent it from those things which it finds alluring, fasting was not made obligatory until the second year after the *hijrah*.[1] So when the hearts were fully established upon *Tawheed* and upon honouring that which Allaah has made obligatory, then they were lead to it (fasting) in stages. At first they were given the choice and it was better for them to fast. Since it was something very difficult for the Companions, *radiyallaahu 'anhum*, whoever wanted to refrain from fasting and instead feed a poor person could do so. The Most Kind and Most Merciful says:

$$وَعَلَى ٱلَّذِينَ يُطِيقُونَهُۥ فِدْيَةٌ طَعَامُ مِسْكِينٍ فَمَن تَطَوَّعَ خَيْرًا فَهُوَ خَيْرٌ لَّهُۥ وَأَن تَصُومُواْ خَيْرٌ لَّكُمْ إِن كُنتُمْ تَعْلَمُونَ ۝$$

"And as for those who can fast (with difficulty) they have (a choice either to fast or) to feed a poor person (for every day). But whoever does good of his own accord, it is better for him. And that you fast, it is better for you if only you knew."[2]

---

1. *Hijrah*: migration; in particular the migration of the Prophet from Makkah to Madeenah.

2. Sooratul-Baqarah (2):184

• Whoever is resident in the month then let him fast

Then the *Aayah* which comes after it was sent down, and abrogated it. As we have been told by the two noble companions, 'Abdullaah ibn 'Umar and Salamah ibn al-Akwa', *radiyallaahu 'anhum*, who both said, '*It was abrogated by:*

$$\text{شَهْرُ رَمَضَانَ ٱلَّذِىٓ أُنزِلَ فِيهِ ٱلْقُرْءَانُ هُدًى لِّلنَّاسِ وَبَيِّنَتٍ}$$
$$\text{مِّنَ ٱلْهُدَىٰ وَٱلْفُرْقَانِ فَمَن شَهِدَ مِنكُمُ ٱلشَّهْرَ فَلْيَصُمْهُ وَمَن كَانَ}$$
$$\text{مَرِيضًا أَوْ عَلَىٰ سَفَرٍ فَعِدَّةٌ مِّنْ أَيَّامٍ أُخَرَ يُرِيدُ ٱللَّهُ بِكُمُ ٱلْيُسْرَ}$$
$$\text{وَلَا يُرِيدُ بِكُمُ ٱلْعُسْرَ وَلِتُكْمِلُوا ٱلْعِدَّةَ وَلِتُكَبِّرُوا ٱللَّهَ عَلَىٰ}$$
$$\text{مَا هَدَىٰكُمْ وَلَعَلَّكُمْ تَشْكُرُونَ ﴿١٨٥﴾}$$

"The Month of Ramadaan in which was revealed the Qur'aan, a guidance for mankind and clear proofs for the guidance and the Criterion (between right and wrong). So whoever of you sights (the crescent on the first night of) the month (of Ramadaan), he must fast that month, and whoever is ill or on a journey, the same number (of days which one did not fast must be made up) from other days. Allaah intends for you ease, and He does not want to make things difficult for you. (He wants that you) must complete the same number (of days), and that you must glorify Allaah for having guided you so that you may be grateful to Him."[3]

Ibn Abee Lailaa said: "The Companions of Muhammad (ﷺ) narrated to us: that Ramadaan was sent upon them and it was difficult for them. So those who did not fast fed a poor person for each missed day, and this was an allowance for them, but this was abrogated by:

---

3. The *hadeeth* of Ibn 'Umar is reported by al-Bukhaaree (4/188) and the *hadeeth* of Salamah is reported by al-Bukhaaree (8/181) and Muslim (no. 1445).

$$\text{وَأَن تَصُومُواْ خَيْرٌ لَّكُمْ}$$

"...and if you fast it is better for you"

and they were ordered to fast"[4]

Then, fasting the month of Ramadaan became one of the supports of Islaam and pillars of the *Deen*, due to the saying of the Prophet of mercy and guidance (ﷺ): *"Islaam is built upon five: The testification that none has the right to be worshipped except Allaah and that Muhammad is the Messenger of Allaah, establishment of the Salaah, payment of Zakaah, performing Hajj to the House, and fasting in Ramadaan."*[5]

---

4. Reported in *mu'allaq* form by al-Bukhaaree (8/181 of *al-Fath*) and in connected form by al-Baihaqee in his *Sunan* (4/200) and its *isnaad* is *saheeh*, and Aboo Daawood reports its like but in a longer narration (no. 507).

5. Reported by al-Bukhaaree (1/48) and Muslim (no. 16) from Ibn 'Umar.

Chapter 4

Extreme Encouragement to Fast in Ramadaan

• Forgiveness of sins

The Prophet (ﷺ) urged that one fasts in Ramadaan, explaining its excellence and high station, such that if the fasting person had sins as many as the foam upon the sea, then they would be forgiven for him through this pure and blessed act of worship. From Aboo Hurairah, *radiyallaahu 'anhu*, from the Prophet (ﷺ) who said: *"He who fasts Ramadaan, due to eemaan and hoping for reward (from Allaah) then his previous sins are forgiven."*[1]

From Aboo Hurairah, *radiyallaahu 'anhu*, that the Prophet (ﷺ) climbed upon the *mimbar* (pulpit) and said: *"Aameen [O Allaah grant it], aameen, aameen."* So it was said, "O Messenger of Allaah, you climbed upon the mimbar and said, aameen, aameen, aameen?" So he said: *"Indeed Jibraa'eel, 'alayhis salaam, came to me and said, 'Whoever reaches the month of Ramadaan and does not have [his sins] forgiven and so enters the Fire, then may Allaah distance him, say 'aameen" So I said: "aameen"...."* The *hadeeth*.[2]

---

1. Reported by al-Bukhaaree (4/99) and Muslim (no. 759), and the meaning of the *hadeeth* is one who affirms its obligation and hopes for reward for it, being pleased with it, not having aversion to it, nor thinking that standing in Prayer in its nights is a hardship.

2. It is reported by Ibn Khuzaimah (3/192), Ahmad (2/246,254) and al-Baihaqee (4/204). It is an authentic *hadeeth* and its main part is reported in *Saheeh Muslim* (4/1978).

• That supplication (*du'aa*) is answered and freedom from the Fire is granted

He (ﷺ) said: *"There are in the month of Ramadaan in every day and night those to whom Allaah grants freedom from the Fire, and there is for every Muslim a supplication which he can make and will be granted."*[3]

• He will be amongst the true followers of the prophets and the martyrs

From 'Amr ibn Murrah al-Juhanee, *radiyallaahu 'anhu*, who said: A man came to the Prophet (ﷺ) and said: *"O Messenger of Allaah (ﷺ) what if I testify that none has the right to be worshipped but Allaah and that you are the Messenger of Allaah, and I observe the five daily prayers, and I pay the zakaah, and I fast and stand in prayer in Ramadaan, then amongst whom shall I be?"* He said: *"Amongst the true followers of the prophets and the martyrs."*[4]

---

3. Reported by al-Bazzaar (no. 3142) and Ahmad (2/254) by way of al-A'mash: from Aboo Saalih: from Jaabir. Ibn Maajah reports it (no. 1643) from him in shortened form through a different chain, and it is *saheeh*. And the supplication which is granted is at the time of breaking the fast (*iftaar*) as will follow.

4. Reported by Ibn Hibbaan (no. 19 of *az-Zawaa'id*), and its chain of narration is *saheeh*.

Chapter 5

Warning Against Failing to Fast in Ramadaan

Aboo Umaamah al-Baahilee, *radiyallaahu 'anhu*, said: I heard Allaah's Messenger (🌸) say: *"Whilst I was sleeping two men came to me and took hold of my arms and brought me to a steep mountain and said: 'climb' so I said: 'I am not able to.' So they said: 'We will make it easy for you.' So I climbed until I came to the summit of the mountain where I heard terrible cries, so I said: 'what are these cries?' They said: 'That is the howling of the people of the Fire.' Then they took me further on until I came to a people who were strung up by their hamstrings, with their jawbones torn and flowing with blood, so I said: 'who are these.' He said: 'Those who break their fast before the time at which they may do so.'"*[1]

As for what is reported that the Prophet (🌸) said: *"He who deliberately fails to fast a day of Ramadaan - even if he were to fast forever it would not make up for it."*

This *hadeeth* is weak (*da'eef*), not authentic, as will be explained in detail later, *inshaallaah*.

---

1. Reported by an-Nasaa'ee in *al-Kubraa*, as occurs in *Tuhfatul-'Ashraaf* (4/166), Ibn Hibbaan and al-Haakim (1/430). Its chain of narration is *saheeh*.

Chapter 6

The Regulations for Fasting

O Muslim, servant of Allaah, may Allaah increase us all in knowledge, know that this huge reward and great benefit which cannot be enumerated except by the Most Forgiving, the Most Merciful, will not be reached except by one who fasts Ramadaan in accordance with what the final Prophet (ﷺ) established in the *Sunnah* and explained - those rulings connected to this great obligation and this blessed month.

So here we will explain them: not blindly following opinions unsupported by proof, rather taking from the Magnificent Qur'aan, and what is *saheeh* and *hasan*[1] from the pure Sunnah - understood according to the understanding of our pious predecessors, the four *imaams*, and those before them - the Companions and those who followed their way, and this is sufficient proof for you. From the views of the scholars we have chosen the most correct and the best of their sayings.

---

1. For definition of these terms refer to Glossary.

Chapter 7

At the Approach of Ramadaan

• Counting the days of Sha'baan[1]

The Muslim *Ummah*[2] should count the days from the beginning of Sha'baan in preparation for Ramadaan, since any month will be either twenty-nine or thirty days long. So if the new moon is seen, then one must fast and if that is not possible due to clouds, then thirty days of Sha'baan are to be completed. Allaah, the Originator of the heavens and the earth made the appearance of the new moon a sign for the people to be able to keep account of years, months and days, and a month cannot be longer than thirty days.

From Aboo Hurairah, *radiyallaahu 'anhu*, who said: Allaah's Messenger (ﷺ) said: *"Fast when it (the moon) is seen and cease fasting when it is seen, so if it is concealed by clouds, then complete thirty days of Sha'baan."*[3]

From 'Abdullaah ibn 'Umar, *radiyallaahu 'anhumaa*, that Allaah's Messenger (ﷺ) said: *"Do not fast until you see the new moon and do not cease fasting until you see it, and if it is concealed by clouds then count out (the days of Sha'baan) for it."*[4]

---

1. The eighth month of the Islamic calendar (the one preceding Ramadaan).

2. *Ummah*: Nation.

3. Reported by al-Bukhaaree (4/106) and Muslim (no. 1081).

4. Reported by al-Bukhaaree (4/120) and Muslim (no. 1080).

From 'Adiyy ibn Haatim, *radiyallaahu 'anhu*, who said: He (ﷺ) said: *"When Ramadaan comes to you then fast thirty (days) unless you see the new moon before that."*[5]

• Forbiddance of fasting on the day of doubt

A Muslim should not precede Ramadaan by fasting a day or two before it, thinking that it might be Ramadaan, unless that occurs on a day which he is accustomed to fasting.

From Aboo Hurairah, *radiyallaahu 'anhu*, who said: He (ﷺ) said: *"Do not pre-empt Ramadaan by fasting a day or two before it, except for a man fasting his usual fast - then let him fast it."*[6]

So be aware, O brother in Islaam, that whoever fasts the day about which there is doubt has disobeyed Allaah's Messenger (ﷺ). Silah ibn Zufar reports from 'Ammaar: *"Whoever fasts the day about which there is doubt has disobeyed Abul-Qaasim (ﷺ)."*[7]

---

5. Reported by at-Tahaawee in *Mushkilul-Aathaar* (no. 501), Ahmad (4/377) and at-Tabaraanee in *al-Kabeer* (17/171). Its *isnaad* contains Mujaalid ibn Sa'eed who is weak as al-Haithumee says in *Majma'uz-Zawaa'id* (3/146), however the *hadeeth* has a number of supports which can be seen in *al-Irwaa'* (no. 901) of our Shaikh al-Albaanee, *hafidhahullaah*.

6. Reported by Muslim.

7. Reported in *mu'allaq* form by al-Bukhaaree (4/119), connected by Aboo Daawood (no. 3334), at-Tirmidhee (no. 686), an-Nasaa'ee (no. 2188) and Ibn Maajah (no. 3334). Its *isnaad* contains Aboo Ishaaq as-Sabee'ee who is a *mudallis* who has performed *'an'anah*. His memory also deteriorated at the end of his life, however it has other chains and supports which are quoted by Ibn Hajr in *Taghleequt Ta'leeq* (3/141-142) which make the *hadeeth hasan*.

• Sighting the moon

Appearance of the new moon is confirmed by the witness of two reliable Muslims, as he (ﷺ) said: *"Fast when it is seen, and cease fasting when it is seen and perform the rites of Hajj based upon that and if it is hidden by clouds then complete thirty (days), and if two witnesses testify then fast and cease fasting."*[8]

It will not pass unnoticed that just because two witnesses are accepted in one case does not mean that a single witness cannot be accepted, rather the witness of a single person that has seen the new moon is acceptable, for it is established that Ibn 'Umar, *radiyallaahu 'anhumaa*, said: *"The people looked out for the new moon, so I informed the Prophet (ﷺ) that I had seen it, so he fasted and ordered the people to fast."*[9]

---

8. Reported by an-Nasaa'ee (4/132), Ahmad (4/321), and ad-Daaraqutnee. Its chain of narration is *hasan*. This wording is an-Nasaa'ee's, Ahmad adds: *two Muslim witnesses*, and ad-Daaraqutnee has: *reliable*.

9. Reported by Aboo Daawood (no. 2342), ad-Daarimee (2/4), Ibn Hibbaan (no. 871), al-Haakim (1/423) and al-Baihaqee (4/212). Its chain of narration is *saheeh* as al-Haafidh Ibn Hajr says in *at-Talkheesul-Habeer* (2/187).

Chapter 8

The Intention (*An-Niyyah*)

• The obligation to have intention for the obligatory fast before the appearance of the true dawn

When it is confirmed that the month of Ramadaan has commenced, either by seeing the moon, or through someone's witness, or through completion of the number (i.e. thirty days of Sha'baan) then it is obligatory upon every Muslim upon whom the *Sharee'ah* rulings are binding to intend to fast until the night, as he (ﷺ) said: *"He who does not resolve to fast before it is Fajr, then there is no fast for him."*[1]

He (ﷺ) also said: *"He who does not intend during the night to fast, then there is no fast for him."*[2]

The place for the intention is the heart, to pronounce it upon the tongue is an innovation (*bid'ah*) and misguidance - even if the people think it to be good. The necessity of having intention from the night is particular to obligatory fasts since the Messenger (ﷺ) used to come to 'Aa'ishah, *radiyallaahu 'anhaa*, at

---

1. Reported by Aboo Daawood (no. 2454), Ibn Khuzaimah (no. 1933), al-Baihaqee (4/202), an-Nasaa'ee (4/196) and at-Tirmidhee (no. 730). Its *isnaad* is *saheeh*.

2. Reported by an-Nasaa'ee (4/196), al-Baihaqee (4/202) and Ibn Hazm (6/162). Its *isnaad* would be *saheeh* were it not for the *'an'anah* of Ibn Juraij, but is indeed *saheeh* due to the previous narration.

times other than Ramadaan and say: *"Do you have any food? If not, then I am fasting."*[3]

The like of this is reported from the practice of the Companions: Abud-Dardaa', Aboo Talhah, Aboo Hurairah, Ibn 'Abbaas and Hudhaifah ibn al-Yamaan, *radiyallaahu 'anhum*, and may Allaah raise us up amongst them beneath the flag of the noblest of the children of Aadam (ﷺ).[4]

So this refers to the optional fast and shows that the obligation of having intention before the appearance of the true dawn is for the obligatory fast - and Allaah the Most High knows best.

• Obligation and requirement depends upon one being able

As for a person who enters upon Ramadaan but doesn't know, so he eats and drinks, such a person should withhold from eating and drinking and complete his fast as soon as he becomes aware (that it is Ramadaan) - and it counts for him. As for one who has not eaten then he should not eat, and having intention from the night is not a condition in his case since he is unable to do that, and one of the well known principles of the *Sharee'ah* is that obligation and requirement depend upon a person's ability.

'Aa'ishah, *radiyallaahu 'anhaa*, said: *"Allaah's Messenger (ﷺ) used to order fasting on the day of 'Aashooraa,[5] when Ramadaan become obligatory it became the case that whoever wanted fasted, and whoever wanted refrained from fasting [that day]."*[6]

---

3. Reported by Muslim (no. 1154)

4. To see these narrations and their sources refer to *Taghleequt-Ta'leeq* (3/144-147).

5. **Publisher's note:** Aashooraa is the 10th. of Muharram. See *Saheeh al-Bukhaaree* (eng. trans., vol. 3, no. 222)

6. Reported by al-Bukhaaree (4/212) and Muslim (no. 1125).

From Salamah ibn al-Akwa', *radiyallahu 'anhu*, who said: *"The Prophet (ﷺ) ordered a man of the tribe of Aslam to call out amongst the people that whoever has eaten then let him fast for the rest of the day, and whoever has not eaten - then let him fast, because the day is 'Aashooraa."*[7]

So this day of 'Aashooraa was obligatory, then (later) its obligation was abrogated - and they had been ordered to cease eating in the day and that sufficed for them, and Ramadaan is obligatory, and the ruling for the obligatory action does not change.

• Some scholars disagree and say that such a person has to make up that fast later

Some scholars hold that fasting 'Aashooraa was not obligatory. But know, O brother in *eemaan*, that the proofs when taken together show that the fast of 'Aashooraa was indeed obligatory. This is shown by the order affirmed in the *hadeeth* of 'Aa'ishah, then the order was strengthened by further affirmation in the form of the general proclamation, then further affirmed by the order that one who had already eaten should withhold, as occurs in the *hadeeth* of Salamah ibn al-Akwa' and that of Muhammad ibn Saifee al-Ansaaree who said: *"Allaah's Messenger (ﷺ) came out to us on the day of 'Aashooraa and said: 'Are you fasting on this day of yours?' So some of them said, 'yes', and some said, 'no'. He said, 'Then complete the rest of this day of yours.' And he ordered them to announce to the people of the towns around al-Madeenah, that they should complete the rest of the day."*[8]

The recommendation of fasting on the day of 'Aashooraa remains - indeed there is *ijmaa'* (total consensus) that it is recommended as al-Haafidh reports in *al-Fath* (4/246) from Ibn 'Abdul-Barr. So it is certain that it remains, which shows that what was abrogated was its obligation - and Allaah knows best.

---

7. Reported by al-Bukhaaree (4/216) and Muslim (no. 1135).

8. Reported by Ibn Khuzaimah (3/389), Ahmad (4/388), an-Nasaa'ee (4/192), Ibn Maajah (1/552) and at-Tabaraanee in *al-Kabeer* (18/238). Its *isnaad* is *saheeh*.

Others say: If it was obligatory then it has been abrogated, and the rulings attached to it have also been abrogated. But the truth is that the *ahaadeeth* about 'Aashooraa indicate various points:

(a) The obligation of the fast of 'Aashooraa'
(b) That one who does not have intention to keep obligatory fast from before the appearance of dawn due to his being unaware - then this does not destroy his fast.
(c) That one who eats and drinks, then comes to know, should withhold for the rest of the day and does not have to make up for that fast.

What is abrogated from them is the first point, (a), and it became something recommended as has preceded - and the fact that this is abrogated does not mean that the other rulings are abrogated - and Allaah knows best.

They also use as evidence a *hadeeth* reported by Aboo Daawood (no. 2447) and Ahmad (5/409), by way of Qataadah: from 'Abdur-Rahmaan ibn Salamah: from his uncle: That Aslam came to the Prophet (ﷺ) so he said: *"Are you fasting this day of yours?' They said: 'No.' He said: 'Then complete the rest of this day of yours and repeat it.'"*

However this *hadeeth* is *da'eef* (weak) containing two weaknesses:

(i) The fact that 'Abdur-Rahmaan ibn Salamah is unknown. Adh-Dhahabee says of him in *al-Meezaan* (2/567): "He is not known." Al-Haafidh says in *at-Tahdheeb* (6/239): "His condition is unknown." Ibn Abee Haatim mentions him in *al-Jarh wat-Ta'deel* (5/288) and doesn't say anything for or against him.

(ii) It contains the *'an'anah* of Qataadah who is a *mudallis*.

Chapter 9

The Time for Beginning and Ending the Fast

When the Companions of the unlettered Prophet Muhammad (ﷺ) fasted and the time for breaking the fast came, then they would eat, drink and cohabit with their wives as long as they didn't fall asleep. If one of them fell asleep before eating the evening meal then it was not permissible to do any of that until the next evening. Then the Mercy of their Lord, the All-Powerful, the Bestower, enveloped them and allowance was made for them, and they were overjoyed - this is explained in the following *hadeeth*:

From al-Baraa', *radiyallaahu 'anhu*, who said: *"When the companions of the Prophet (ﷺ) fasted and it became time to break the fast, if one of them slept before eating, then he would not eat that night, nor the next day until evening. Once Qays ibn Sirmah al-Ansaaree was fasting, so when it was time to break the fast he came to his wife and said to her, 'Do you have any food?' She said: 'No, but I will go and seek some for you.' He used to work during the day so sleep overtook him, then his wife came and when she saw him she said, 'You have missed it.' Then in the middle of the next day he fainted, and that was mentioned to the Prophet(ﷺ), so this Aayah was sent down:*

$$\text{أُحِلَّ لَكُمْ لَيْلَةَ ٱلصِّيَامِ ٱلرَّفَثُ إِلَىٰ نِسَآئِكُمْ}$$

"It is made lawful for you to have sexual relations with your wives on the night of the fasts." [1]

---

1. Sooratul-Baqarah (2):187

So they were overjoyed, and,

$$\text{وَكُلُواْ وَٱشْرَبُواْ حَتَّىٰ يَتَبَيَّنَ لَكُمُ ٱلْخَيْطُ ٱلْأَبْيَضُ مِنَ ٱلْخَيْطِ ٱلْأَسْوَدِ مِنَ ٱلْفَجْرِ}$$

"And eat and drink until the white thread (light) of dawn appears to you distinct from the black thread (darkness of night)."[2]
was also sent down."[3]

This is the cherishing mercy which the Most Kind and Most Merciful gives abundantly to His humble servants who say: *We hear and we obey, we ask for Your forgiveness our Lord, and to you we return.*[4]

The fast has a specified time - with specified beginning and end - and is from the appearance of Fajr until the daytime ends, the night begins and the suns disc is hidden by the horizon.

• The white thread and the black thread

When the aforementioned *Aayah* was sent down, some of the Companions of the Prophet (ﷺ) took black camel tethers and white ones and placed them beneath their pillows, or (one) tied them to his foot and would continue eating and drinking until he could distinguish them.

From 'Adiyy ibn Haatim , *radiyallaahu 'anhu*, who said: *"When,*

$$\text{حَتَّىٰ يَتَبَيَّنَ لَكُمُ ٱلْخَيْطُ ٱلْأَبْيَضُ مِنَ ٱلْخَيْطِ ٱلْأَسْوَدِ}$$

"Until the white thread appears to you distinct from the black thread"[5]

---

2. Sooratul-Baqarah (2):187

3. Reported by al-Bukhaaree (4/911).

4. See Qur'aan, Sooratul-Baqarah (2):285

5. Sooratul-Baqarah (2):187

was sent down I took a black and a white camel tether and placed them beneath my pillow, and during the night I would look to see but they didn't appear any different to each other, so in the morning I went to the Prophet (ﷺ) and informed him, so he said: 'Rather it is the blackness of night and the whiteness of dawn.'"[6]

From Sahl ibn Sa'd, *radiyallaahu 'anhu*, who said: *"When this Aayah was sent down:*

"And eat and drink until the white thread appears to you distinct from the black thread."[7]

a man wanting to fast would tie a black thread to one foot and a white thread to the other, and would continue eating and drinking until he could tell one from the other, then afterwards Allaah sent down:

مِنَ ٱلْفَجْرِ

"from the dawn"

so they knew that what was meant (by the black thread and the white thread) was the night and the day."[8]

---

6. Reported by al-Bukhaaree (4/113) and Muslim (no. 1090). The narration apparently shows that 'Adiyy was present when this *Aayah* was sent down, which means that he was a Muslim at the time. However this is not the case, since fasting was made obligatory in the second year after the Hijrah, and 'Adiyy accepted Islaam in the ninth or tenth year as occurs in *al-Isaabah* (2/468). So either we say that the *Aayah* was sent down very much later on and this is very unlikely, or that we explain the saying of 'Adiyy: *When it was sent down,* to mean *When I accepted Islaam and this Aayah was recited to me.* And this is what is correct due to the narration of Ahmad in his *Musnad* (4/377): "Allaah's Messenger (ﷺ) taught me the prayer and fasting, he said: 'Pray such and such, and fast and when the sun sets then eat and drink until the white thread is clear to you from the black thread, and fast for thirty days unless you see the new moon before that so I took two threads of wool, one black and one white... (the *hadeeth*).'" abridged from *Fathul-Baaree* (4/132-133).

7. Sooratul-Baqarah (2):187

8. Reported by al-Bukhaaree (4/114) and Muslim (no. 1091).

After this Qur'aanic explanation, the Messenger (ﷺ) clearly explained to his companions exactly what was intended, with a clear description leaving no room for doubt or ignorance.

• The two fajrs

So from these regulations which Allaah's Messenger (ﷺ) explained in detail is that there are two fajrs:

(i) The False dawn (al-Fajrul-Kaadhib) - which does not make it lawful to pray the Fajr prayer, nor does it prohibit eating for one intending to fast.

(ii) The true dawn (al-Fajrus-Saadiq) - which is the one which makes food forbidden for the fasting person, and makes Fajr prayer lawful.

From Ibn 'Abbaas, radiyallaahu 'anhumaa, who said: Allaah's Messenger (ﷺ) said: "The Fajr is two Fajrs: As for the first then it does not make food forbidden, nor does it make the prayer lawful. As for the second, then it makes food forbidden and the prayer lawful."9

(1) The False Fajr is the rising vertical column of whiteness which appears looking like the tail of a fox.

(2) The True Fajr is the horizontally spreading reddishness which can be seen above the mountain passes and mountain tops, which spreads its light throughout the roads, streets, and houses - and it is this one upon which the rulings of fasting and prayer depend.

---

9. Reported by Ibn Khuzaimah (3/210), al-Haakim (1/191-495), ad-Daaraqutnee (2/165) and al-Baihaqee (4/261) by way of Sufyaan: from Ibn Juraij: From 'Ataa: From Ibn 'Abbaas and its isnaad is saheeh. It has a supporting witness from Jaabir reported by al-Haakim (1/191), al-Baihaqee (4/215) and ad-Daaraqutnee (2/165) and they differ about its being mawsool or mursal, and it has a third witnessing narration from Thawbaan reported by Ibn Abee Shaibah (3/27).

From Samurah, *radiyallaahu 'anhu*, who said: Allaah's Messenger (ﷺ) said: *"Let not the adhaan of Bilaal deceive you, nor this vertical whiteness of dawn until it spreads horizontally."*[10]

From Talq ibn 'Alee: that the Prophet (ﷺ) said: *"Eat and drink and do not let the tall vertical brightness deceive you, but eat and drink until the reddish one spreads horizontally for you."*[11]

Know - O one who has been guided to obedience to his Lord, that the descriptions of the true fajr agree with the noble *Aayah*:

$$حَتَّىٰ يَتَبَيَّنَ لَكُمُ ٱلْخَيْطُ ٱلْأَبْيَضُ مِنَ ٱلْخَيْطِ ٱلْأَسْوَدِ مِنَ ٱلْفَجْرِ$$

"Until the white thread (light) of dawn appears to you distinct from the black thread (darkness of night)..."[12]

Since the light of fajr when it spreads over the mountain passes and mountain tops appears like a white thread, and a black thread appears above it - and this is the remnants of the darkness which is passing away.

So when this becomes clear to you then withhold from eating, drinking and sexual intercourse, and if there is cup of water or a drink in your hand then drink it at ease since it is a great allowance from the Most Merciful of the merciful for His fasting servants, even if you hear the *adhaan*. He (ﷺ) said: *"If one of you hears the call and the drinking vessel is in his hand then let him not put it down until he has satisfied his need from it."*[13]

---

10. Reported by Muslim (no. 1094).

11. Reported by at-Tirmidhee (3/76), Aboo Daawood (2/304), Ahmad (4/23) and Ibn Khuzaimah (3/211). Its *isnaad* is *saheeh*.

12. Sooratul-Baqarah (2):187

13. Reported by Aboo Daawood (no. 235), Ahmad (2/423), al-Haakim (1/426), al-Baihaqee (2/218) and Ibn Jareer (no. 3115) from Aboo Hurairah. Its *isnaad* is *hasan*, and it has another chain of narration reported by Ahmad (2/510) and al-Haakim (1/203,205) and it is *saheeh*.

What is meant by the call (an-Nidaa) is the second adhaan given for the appearance of the true dawn, as is shown by the additional wording reported by Ahmad (2/510), Ibn Jareer at-Tabaree (2/102) and others at the end of the hadeeth: "...and the mu'adhdhin used to give the adhaan when the dawn appeared."

This meaning is attested to by what Aboo Umaamah, radiyallaahhu 'anhu, reports: "That the call for prayer was given and a drinking vessel was in the hand of 'Umar, so he said: 'shall I drink it, O Messenger of Allaah?' He said: 'yes,' so he drank it."[14]

So it is confirmed that withholding from food before the appearance of the true Fajr due to claims of taking precaution is a novelty and an innovation (bid'ah).

Al-Haafidh [Ibn Hajr], rahimahullaah, says in al-Fath (4/199): "One of the reprehensible innovations which have appeared in this time is to make the secondary adhaan about a third of an hour before fajr in Ramadaan, and the extinguishing of lights which is used as a sign indicating the forbiddance of eating and drinking for one intending to fast, claiming that what he has innovated is a precautionary measure to protect his worship - something not known except by a few individuals. This has lead them to the stage, where they do not give adhaan until four minutes or so after the actual sunset, to make sure of the time as they claim. So they delay breaking the fast and take suhoor early and act in contradiction to the Sunnah, therefore there is little good found in them and much evil, and Allaah's aid is sought."

The innovation of withholding before the appearance of fajr and waiting a certain period of time (at sunset) is still upheld today - it is to Allaah that we complain of our grief.

---

14. Reported by Ibn Jareer (2/102) through two chains from him.

• Then fast until the night

So when night approaches from the direction of the east, and the daylight passes away in the direction of the west, and the sun sets then the person breaks the fast. From 'Umar, *radiyallaahu 'anhu*, who said: He (ﷺ) said: *"When the night approaches from here, and the day passes away from here, and the sun sets, then the fasting persons fast is broken."*[15]

This is something which comes about immediately after the sun sets, even if the light from it is bright and clear, since it was his (ﷺ) practice that when he was fasting he would order a man to climb upon something and when he said that the sun had set, then he would break the fast.[16]

Some people may think that the night does not appear directly after the setting of the sun, but rather starts when the darkness spreads in the east and west. This was also the case with some of the Companions of the Prophet (ﷺ), so they were made aware that the beginning of darkness in the east directly after the sun disappears is sufficient.

From 'Abdullaah ibn Abee Awfaa, *radiyallaahu 'anhu*, who said: *"We were with Allaah's Messenger (ﷺ) on a journey and he was fasting (in the month of Ramadaan), so when the sun set he said to one of the people, 'O so and so (and in a narration of Aboo Daawood: O Bilaal:) stand and mix gruel for us.' He said: 'O Messenger of Allaah if you were to wait until evening'* (and in a narration of al-Bukhaaree: 'The sun!') *He said: 'Get down and mix gruel for us.' He said: 'It is still day time!' He said: 'Get down and mix gruel for us.' So he dismounted and made the gruel, and the Prophet (ﷺ) drank (and he said: 'if anyone had mounted his camel to try and see the sun, he would have seen it'. Then he beckoned* (in a narration of al-Bukhaaree: *'he indicated with his hand')*, (and in a narration of

---

15. Reported by al-Bukhaaree (4/171) and Muslim (no. 1100).

16. Reported by al-Haakim (1/434) and Ibn Khuzaimah (no. 2061). Al-Haakim declared it to be authentic to the standard of al-Bukhaaree and Muslim.

al-Bukhaaree and Muslim: 'he indicated with his finger towards the east') then said: 'when you see that the night has approached from here then the fasting person's fast is broken.'"[17]

It is confirmed that the Companions of the Prophet (ﷺ) complied with him (ﷺ) in their actions. It is reported that Aboo Sa'eed al-Khudree used to break his fast as soon as the disc of the sun disappeared.[18]

The rulings connected with fasting which have just been explained are determined by seeing with the naked eye. It is not right that one should overburden oneself needlessly by seeking out the moon and the time of fajr by use of newly invented astronomical devices, or by clinging to timetables of the people of astronomy which have enticed the Muslims away from the Sunnah of the Seal of the Prophets (ﷺ) - so that little good is found in them and much evil[19] - and Allaah knows best.

In some Muslim lands the mu'adhdhins use timetables which are over fifty years old! So they delay the breaking of the fast, make the suhoor very early and fall into direct contradiction to the guidance of the Prophet (ﷺ). So some of those anxious to follow the Sunnah break their fast when they see the sun set, and end suhoor when the true dawn appears - as has preceded, so this is what is correct in the Sharee'ah. Whoever thinks that this is incorrect, then he has committed a very great error and there is no movement except by the will of Allaah.

---

17. Reported by al-Bukhaaree (4/199), Muslim (no. 1101), Ahmad (4/381) and Aboo Daawood (no. 2352). The first addition is reported by Muslim (no. 1101) and the second by 'Abdur-Razzaaq (4/226). The hadeeth contains many valuable points which can be seen in al-Fath (4/198).

18. Reported by al-Bukhaaree in mu'allaq form (4/196) and is connected by Ibn Abee Shaibah in al-Musannaf (3/12).

19. A fuller explanation can be found in the following books:
(i) Majmoo'ul-Fataawaa of Shaikh-ul-Islaam Ibn Taimiyyah (25/126-202)
(ii) Al-Majmoo' (6/279) of an-Nawawee, and,
(ii) At-Talkheesul-Habeer (2/187-188) of Ibn Hajr.

So it is clear that this act of worship is determined by the sun and the fajr, and if any people differ, then they are the ones upon error, not those who cling to and remain upon the original state of affairs. The *adhaan* is the proclamation that the time has begun, so if the time is reached and the adhaan is delayed, or if the *adhaan* is given early then one should remain upon the original way, and that is what is obligatory - so remember this and ponder over it!

Chapter 10

The Pre-Dawn Meal *(Suhoor)*

• Its wisdom

Allaah has made fasting obligatory upon us, just as it was prescribed for the People of the Book before us. Allaah, the Most High says:

$$كُتِبَ عَلَيْكُمُ ٱلصِّيَامُ كَمَا كُتِبَ عَلَى ٱلَّذِينَ مِن قَبْلِكُمْ لَعَلَّكُمْ تَتَّقُونَ ﴿١٨٣﴾$$

"...Fasting is prescribed for you as it was prescribed for those before you, that you may become pious."[1]

Originally the time of fasting and its rulings were in accordance with what was prescribed for the People of the Book. It was not permissible to eat, drink or have sexual intercourse after one had slept meaning that if one fell asleep before eating then he could not eat until the next evening, and this was also prescribed for the Muslims as has preceded.[2]

When this was abrogated Allaah's Messenger (ﷺ) ordered the taking of *suhoor* as a distinction between our fast and that of the People of the Book.

---

1. Sooratul-Baqarah (2):183

2. For further details refer to the following books of *tafseer*:
(i) *Zaadul-Maseer* (1/184) of Ibn al-Jawzee,
(ii) *Tafseerul-Qur'aan al-Adheem* (1/213-214) of Ibn Katheer, and,
(iii) *ad-Durrul-Manthoor* (1/120-121) of as-Suyootee.

37

From 'Amr ibn al-'Aas, *radiyallaahu 'anhu*, that Allaah's Messenger (ﷺ) said: *"The distinction between our fasting and the fasting of the People of the Book is the taking of the pre-dawn meal (suhoor)."*3

• Its excellence

From Salmaan, *radiyallaahu 'anhu*, who said: He (ﷺ) said: *"Blessing is in three: the Jamaa'ah, ath-thareed [a broth of (crumbled) bread and meat] and the suhoor."*4

From Aboo Hurairah, *radiyallaahu 'anhu*, who said: He (ﷺ) said: *"Indeed Allaah placed blessing in the suhoor and in the weighing [of grain]."*5

From 'Abdullaah ibn al-Haarith, from a man of the Companions of the Prophet (ﷺ) who said: *"I entered upon the Prophet (ﷺ) and he was taking the suhoor and he said: 'It is a blessing which Allaah has given to you, so do not leave it.'"*6

It is clear that the *suhoor* is a blessing since it is compliance to the *Sunnah*. It strengthens a person for fasting and increases his desire to fast more often because fasting is made easier by it (*suhoor*) and it involves acting contrary to the People of the Book, for they do not take *suhoor*. Therefore, the noble Messenger (ﷺ) called it the blessed morning meal as occurs in the *hadeeth* of al-'Irbaad ibn Saariyah and Abud-Dardaa', *radiyallaahu 'anhumaa*: *"Come to

---

3. Reported by Muslim (no. 1096).

4. Reported by at-Tabaraanee in *al-Kabeer* (no. 6127) and Aboo Nu'aim in *Dhikr Akhbaar Asbahaan* (1/58) from Salmaan al-Farsee. Al-Haithumee says in *al-Majma'* (3/151): "Its (chain) contains Aboo 'Abdullaah al-Basree of whom adh-Dhahabee says: 'He is not known' and the rest of its narrators are reliable." It has a witnessing narration from Aboo Hurairah, reported by al-Khateeb in *Muwaddih Awhaamul-Jam' wat-Tafreeq* (1/263) and its *isnaad* is *hasan* as a support.

5. Reported by ash-Sheeraazee in *al-Alqaab* as occurs in *al-Jaami' us-Sagheer* (no. 1715) and al-Khateeb in *al-Muwaddih* (1/263) from Aboo Hurairah with the previous *isnaad* which is *hasan* as a support and is itself witnessed to by the previous narration.

6. Reported by Ahmad (5/270) and an-Nasaa'ee (4/145). Its *isnaad* is *saheeh*.

the blessed morning meal (meaning the *suhoor*)."[7]

Perhaps the greatest blessing of *suhoor* is that Allaah, the Most High, free of all imperfections, covers them with His forgiveness and sends His Mercy upon them. The angels of the Most Merciful ask for forgiveness for them, and supplicate to Allaah that He pardons them, so that they may be granted freedom from the Fire by the Most Merciful in the month of the Qur'aan.

From Aboo Sa'eed al-Khudree, *radiyallaahu 'anhu*, who said: He (ﷺ) said: *"The suhoor is a meal of blessings, so do not leave it, even if one of you just takes a (gulp) of water, since Allaah sends mercy and His angels seek forgiveness for those who take the suhoor."*[8]

So the Muslim should not allow this great reward from the Merciful Lord pass him by, and the best form of *suhoor* is dates. He (ﷺ) said: *"How excellent are dates as the believer's suhoor."*[9]

If one does not find dates then let him be careful to take *suhoor*, even if only with a gulp of water due to what we have mentioned, and his (ﷺ) saying: *"Take suhoor even if only with a gulp of water."*[10]

---

7. The *hadeeth* of al-'Irbaad ibn Saariyah is reported by Ahmad (4/126), Aboo Daawood (2/303) and an-Nasaa'ee (4/145). Its isnaad contains al-Haarith ibn Ziyaad who is unknown. The *hadeeth* of Abud-Dardaa' is reported by Ibn Hibbaan (no. 223 of *al-Mawaarid*) and its *isnaad* contains Rishdeen ibn Sa'd who is weak. And it has a further witness from the *hadeeth* of al-Miqdaam ibn Ma'dee Karib - reported by Ahmad (4/133) and an-Nasaa'ee (4/146) and its *isnaad* is saheeh except for Baqiyyah [ibn al-Waleed]. So the *hadeeth* is saheeh.

8. Reported by Ahmad (3/12 and 44) and Ibn Abee Shaibah (3/8) and its *isnaads* support each other.

9. Reported by Aboo Daawood (2/303), Ibn Hibban (no. 223) and al-Baihaqee (4/237). Its *isnaad* is saheeh.

10. Reported by Ahmad (3/12 and 44) and Ibn Abee Shaibah (3/8) and its *isnaads* support each other.

• Delaying the *suhoor*

It is recommended to delay the *suhoor* until just before *fajr* since the Prophet (ﷺ) and Zayd ibn Thaabit, *radiyallaahu 'anhu*, took *suhoor* and when they finished their *suhoor* the Prophet (ﷺ) stood up for the Prayer and prayed. The time between the end of their *suhoor* and their starting the [obligatory] prayer was enough for a person to recite fifty *Aayahs* from the Book of Allaah. Anas, *radiyallaahu 'anhu*, reports from Zayd Ibn Thaabit that he said: *"We ate suhoor along with the Prophet (ﷺ) then he stood up for the prayer, I said: 'How much time was there between the adhaan and the suhoor?' He said: 'The interval was sufficient to recite fifty Aayaat[11].'"[12]*

Know, O servant of Allaah, may Allaah guide you, that eating, drinking and sexual intercourse is lawful for you as long as you are uncertain of the appearance of *fajr* and it has not become apparent. Since Allaah the Most Majestic and His Messenger (ﷺ) explained that the limit is its becoming apparent, so act accordingly, and He the Most Majestic has pardoned errors and forgetfulness and has allowed eating, drinking and intercourse until it becomes apparent. As for a person who is uncertain then it has not become apparent because its becoming apparent is something certain - containing no doubt, so await its becoming apparent.

---

11. **Translator's note:** meaning the interval between the end of *suhoor* and the start of the obligatory prayer as indicated by the chapter heading given by al-Bukhaaree and by the other narrations of the *hadeeth*.

12. Reported by al-Bukhaaree (4/118) and Muslim (no. 1097). Al-Haafidh says in *al-Fath* (4/138): "One of the habits of the Arabs was to measure their time with their common actions: the time taken to milk a ewe, the time between two milkings of a female camel, the time taken to slaughter a sheep, but Zayd turned away from this usage and instead measured with the time taken for recitation of the Qur'aan, indicating, *radiyallaahu 'anhu*, that this is a time for worship and that their action was reciting and studying the Qur'aan."

40

• Its ruling

Allaah's Messenger (ﷺ) gave an emphatic order for one wishing to fast that he should take *suhoor*, so he (ﷺ) said: *"Whoever wishes to fast then let him take something as suhoor."*[13]

He (ﷺ) said: *"Take suhoor for there is blessing in it."*[14]

Then he (ﷺ) explained the value of *suhoor* to his *Ummah*, saying: *"The distinction between our fasting and the fasting of the People of the Book is the taking of the suhoor."*[15]

He (ﷺ) forbade us to leave it, saying: *"The suhoor is a blessed meal, so do not leave it, even if one of you just takes a gulp of water, since Allaah sends mercy and His angels seek forgiveness for those who take the suhoor."*[16]

He (ﷺ) said: *"Take suhoor even if only with a gulp of water."*[17]

We see that the Prophet's (ﷺ) order is heavily emphasised in three ways:

(a) The order itself;
(b) That it is a sign of the fasting of the Muslims and the distinction

---

13. Reported by Ibn Abee Shaibah (3/8), Ahmad (3/438) and al-Bazzaar (1/465). Its narrator Shareek is weak, however it has a witness in *mursal* form reported by Sa'eed ibn Mansoor in his *Sunan* with the wording: *"Take suhoor even with a morsel"* as pointed out by al-Haafidh in *al-Fath* (4/140).

14. Reported by al-Bukhaaree (4/120) and Muslim (no. 1095) from Anas.

15. Reported by Muslim (no. 1096).

16. Reported by Ibn Abee Shaibah (3/8) and Ahmad (3/12 and 44) through three chains from Aboo Sa'eed al-Khudree, and the chains support one another.

17. Reported by Aboo Ya'laa (no. 3340) from Anas, and it contains weakness but it has a supporting witness from the *hadeeth* of 'Abdullaah ibn 'Amr reported by Ibn Hibbaan (no. 884) which contains the *'an'anah* of Qataadah so the *hadeeth* is *hasan*.

41

between their fast and the fast of others; and

(c) The forbiddance of leaving it.

These are strong indications and clear evidences, yet despite all this al-Haafidh Ibn Hajr reports in *Fathul-Baaree* (4/139) that there is *Ijmaa'* that it is [no more than] a recommendation (*mustahabb*)! Allaah knows best.

Chapter 11

Actions that are to be Avoided While Fasting

Know that the fasting person is the one whose limbs withhold from sins, his tongue from lies, foul speech and falsehood, his stomach from food and drink, and his private parts from sexual intercourse. So if he speaks he says that which will not harm his fast, and if he acts he does actions which will not spoil his fast - so his speech is good and his actions righteous.

This is the fasting that is prescribed; not merely withholding from food, drink and desires. Just as food and drink render it invalid, similarly sins cut off its reward, spoil its fruit and make him the same as a person who has not fasted.

The Prophet (ﷺ) urged the fasting Muslim to display noble manners; to be far from foul speech and evil actions; and abstain from rude and obscene talk. The Muslim is commanded to be far from these evil characteristics all the time, the forbiddance being even stronger whilst he is performing the obligation of fasting. So the Muslim who is fasting must avoid those actions which harm his fast, so that he can attain benefit from his fasting and attain the *taqwaa*[1] which Allaah mentioned:

---

1. **Translator's note:** Ibn Abee Shaibah reports in his *Kitaabul-Eemaan* (no. 99) that the *Taabi'ee* Talq ibn Habeeb was asked to define *taqwaa*, so he said: "*Taqwaa* is acting in obedience to Allaah, hoping for His Mercy upon light from Him, and *taqwaa* is leaving acts of disobedience to Allaah, out of fear of Him, upon light from Him." Declared *saheeh* from him by Shaikh al-Albaanee.

"O you who believe! Fasting is prescribed for you as it was pre-scribed for those before you, that you may become *al-Muttaqoon*."[2]

Fasting is a means of attaining *taqwaa*, since it prevents one from many sins that a person is prone to, as he (ﷺ) said: *"Fasting is a shield."*[3]

This has been explained in the chapter on the *Virtues of Fasting*. O Muslim, here we will mention those evil actions which you must be aware of in order to know that they are bad so that you do not fall into them. It was Allaah who gave someone the wisdom to say: "I have acquainted myself with what is evil not to do evil, but to avoid it, and whoever does not know good from evil will indeed fall into it."

• Falsehood

From Aboo Hurairah, *radiyallaahu 'anhu*, who said: He (ﷺ) said: *"Whoever does not abandon falsehood in word and action then Allaah the Mighty and Majestic has no need*[4] *that he should leave his food and drink."*[5]

• Ignorant and indecent speech

From Aboo Hurairah, *radiyallaahu 'anhu*, who said: He (ﷺ) said: *"Fasting is not (merely abstaining) from eating and drinking, rather it is (abstaining) from ignorant and indecent speech, so if anyone abuses or behaves ignorantly with you, then say:*

---

2. Sooratul-Baqarah (2):183

3. *Saheeh*: Reported by Ahmad, al-Bukhaaree and Muslim as has preceded.

4. **Translator's note:** The meaning being that such a fast is not acceptable to Allaah as occurs in *Fathul-Baaree* (4/117) and *Faidul-Qadeer* (6/223-224).

5. Reported by al-Bukhaaree (4/99).

I am fasting, I am fasting."[6]

A severe warning has come from the Prophet (ﷺ) for one who commits these acts, so the truthful and trusted Messenger who does not speak from his own desire said: *"It may be that a fasting person attains nothing but hunger and thirst from his fasting."*[7]

The reason for this is that one who does these things does not understand the reality of fasting which Allaah has made obligatory upon us, so Allaah punishes him by refusing him the reward.[8] Because of this our Pious Predecessors (as-Salafus-Saalih) make a distinction between the forbiddance that is due to something directly related to the worship[9] - which render it futile, and those things not related to it directly,[10] which do not render it futile.[11]

---

6. Reported by Ibn Khuzaimah (no. 1996) and others. Its *isnaad* is *saheeh*.

7. Reported by Ibn Maajah (1/539), ad-Daarimee (2/211), Ahmad (2/441, 373) and al-Baihaqee (4/270). Its *isnaad* is *saheeh*.

8. See *al-Lu'-Lu' Wal Marjaan Feemattafaqa 'Alaihish-Shaikhaan* (no. 707) and *Riyaadus-Saaliheen* (no. 1215).

9. **Translator's note:** e.g. eating and drinking.

10. **Translator's note:** e.g. falsehood.

11. Refer to *Jaami' ul-'Uloom wal-Hikam* (p. 58) of Ibn Rajab.

Chapter 12

Actions that are Permitted While Fasting

Any obedient servant who understands the Book and the *Sunnah* will never doubt the fact that Allaah wishes ease for His servants and not hardship, since He has allowed various things for the fasting person and has eliminated any harm if they are done, and here they are with their proofs:

• That the Fasting person can begin fasting whilst in the state of *janaabah*[1]

It was his (ﷺ) practice that if he was in a state of *janaabah* from his wives when dawn broke he would take a bath after the break of dawn and fast. From 'Aa'ishah and Umm Salamah, *radiyallaahu 'anhumaa: "That sometimes the Prophet(ﷺ) was in a state of Janaabah from his wives and Fajr came upon him, then he would bathe and fast."*[2]

• Use of the Tooth-Stick (*As-Siwaak*)

He (ﷺ) said: *"If it were not that I would be putting my nation to hardship I would have ordered them to use the siwaak along with every wudoo'."*[3]

---

1. Requiring a bath due to sexual intercourse.

2. Reported by al-Bukhaaree (4/123) and Muslim (no.1109).

3. Reported by al-Bukhaaree (2/311) and Muslim (no. 252) with its like.

The Messenger (ﷺ) did not exclude the fasting person from this. So this shows that use of the *siwaak* is for the fasting person and others along with every *wudoo'* and every prayer.[4] Likewise it is not restricted to a particular time, rather it applies before or after midday - and Allaah knows best.

• Washing the mouth and nose

He (ﷺ) used to wash his mouth and nose whilst fasting, but he prevented the fasting person from doing it strongly. He (ﷺ) said: *"...and breath water into you nose strongly unless you are fasting."*[5]

• Embracing and kissing

It is established that 'Aa'ishah, *radiyallaahu 'anhaa*, said: *"Allaah's Messenger (ﷺ) used to kiss and embrace [his wives] while he was fasting, and he had more power to control his desires than any of you."*[6]

However this is something disapproved of for younger men in particular, not for old men, since 'Abdullaah ibn 'Amr ibn al-'Aas reports: *"We were with the Prophet (ﷺ) when a youth came and said, 'May I kiss whilst I am fasting?' He said: 'No.' Then an old man came and said, 'May I kiss whilst I am fasting?' He said, 'Yes.' So we began looking at one another, so Allaah's Messenger (ﷺ) said, 'The old man is able to control himself.'"*[7]

---

4. This is the view of al-Bukhaaree, *rahimahullaah*, Ibn Khuzaimah and others. Refer to *Fathul-Baaree* (4/158), *Saheeh Ibn Khuzaimah* (3/247) and *Sharhus-Sunnah* (6/298).

5. Reported by Ahmad (4/32), Aboo Daawood (2/308), at-Tirmidhee (3/146), an-Nasaa'ee (no. 87), Ibn Maajah (no. 408) and Ibn Abee Shaibah (3/101) from Laqeet ibn Sabrah. Its *isnaad* is *saheeh*.

6. Reported by al-Bukhaaree (4/131) and Muslim (no. 1106).

7. Reported by Ahmad (2/185, 221). Its *isnaad* is weak due to the weakness of Ibn Lahee'ah, but it has a supporting witness reported by at-Tabaraanee in *al-Kabeer* (no. 11040) - its chain contains Habeeb ibn Abee Thaabit who is a *mudallis* and reports here with *'an'anah*. It is therefore *hasan* - refer to *al-Faqeeh wal-Mutafaqqih* (PP. 192-193) as it brings further chains of narration for it.

• Giving blood and injections which do not provide nourishment

This is not one of the things which break the fast. Also refer to the coming section on those things which do break the fast.

• Cupping / blood-letting for medical purposes

This used to be one of those things which broke the fast, then this was abrogated. It is established that the Prophet (ﷺ) had it done whilst fasting - due to the report of Ibn 'Abbaas, *radiyallaahu 'anhumaa*, that the Prophet (ﷺ) was cupped whilst fasting.[8]

• Tasting food

This is with the condition that it does not reach the throat, due to the report from Ibn 'Abbaas, *radiyallaahu 'anhumaa*, who said: *"There is no harm for a person to taste vinegar or anything whilst he is fasting as long as it does not enter his throat."*[9]

• Using *Kuhl*[10] and similar things which enter the eyes

These are things which do not break the fast whether or not they produce a taste in the throat. This was the conclusion preferred by Shaikhul-Islaam Ibn Taymiyyah in his important treatise *Haqeeqatus-Siyaam* and also by his student Ibn Qayyim al-Jawziyyah in his valuable book *Zaadul-Ma'aad*. Imaam al-

---

8. Reported by al-Bukhaaree (4/155) and see: *Naasikhul-Hadeeth wa Mansookhuhu* (pp. 334-338) of Ibn Shaaheen.

9. Reported in *mu'allaq* form by al-Bukhaaree (4/154) and in connected form by Ibn Abee Shaibah (3/47) and al-Baihaqee (4/261) through two chains from him and it is *hasan* - see *Taghleequt-Ta'leeq* (3/151-152).

10. A black substance applied to the rims of the eyelids.

Bukhaaree says in his *Saheeh*: "...Anas, al-Hasan and Ibraaheem did not see any harm in use of *kuhl* for the fasting person."[11]

• Pouring cold water over the head, and taking a bath

Al-Bukhaaree says in his *Saheeh*:[12]

"Chapter: A fasting persons taking a bath:

*And Ibn 'Umar, radiyallaahu 'anhumaa, soaked a garment in water and put it over himself whilst he was fasting, and ash-Sha'bee entered the bath-house whilst he was fasting, and al-Hasan said: 'There is no harm in rinsing the mouth and cooling ones body with cold water when fasting.' And the Prophet (ﷺ) used to pour water over his head whilst fasting due to thirst or the heat."[13]

---

11. *Fathul-Baaree* (4/153). See *Mukhtasar Saheehil-Bukhaaree* (no. 451) of our Shaikh al-Albaanee and *Taghleequt-Ta'leeq* (3/152-153).

12. See previous note.

13. Reported by Ahmad (5/376, 380, 408 and 430) and Aboo Daawood (no. 2365). Its *isnaad* is *saheeh*.

Chapter 13

Allaah Wishes Ease for You

• The traveller

There are authentic *ahaadeeth* reported which show that a traveller has the choice whether to fast or not, and we should not forget that this example of our Lord's Mercy is mentioned in the Noble Book - the Most Merciful, the Bestower of Mercy says:

وَمَن كَانَ مَرِيضًا أَوْ عَلَىٰ سَفَرٍ فَعِدَّةٌ مِّنْ أَيَّامٍ أُخَرَ ۗ يُرِيدُ ٱللَّهُ بِكُمُ ٱلْيُسْرَ وَلَا يُرِيدُ بِكُمُ ٱلْعُسْرَ

"And whoever is ill or on a journey, the same number (of days which one did not fast must be made up) from other days. Allaah intends for you ease, and He does not want to make things difficult for you." [1]

Hamzah ibn 'Amr al-Aslamee asked Allaah's Messenger (ﷺ): *"Shall I fast when travelling?"* and he was a person who fasted often, so Allaah's Messenger (ﷺ) said to him: *"Fast if you wish and refrain from fasting if you wish."* [2]

---

1. Sooratul-Baqarah (2):185

2. Reported by al-Bukhaaree (4/156) and Muslim (no. 1121).

From Anas ibn Maalik, *radiyallaahu 'anhu*, who said: *"I travelled along with Allaah's Messenger (ﷺ) in Ramadaan, and the fasting person would not criticise the one not fasting, nor the one not fasting criticise the fasting person."*[3]

These *ahaadeeth* show that one has a choice, but do not show which is better. It is however possible to show that it is better not to fast from the general *ahaadeeth* such as his (ﷺ) saying: *"Indeed Allaah loves to give allowances, just as He hates that you commit sins."*[4] and in a narration: *"Just as He loves to give His obligations."*[5]

However this may be restricted to refer to one upon whom there is no difficulty in either fasting or making up the fasts later, so that the allowance does not turn into something other than what was intended, and this is clarified by the report of Aboo Sa'eed al-Khudree, *radiyallaahu 'anhu*: *"And they used to hold that one who had the strength and fasted - then that was good, and that he who was weak and refrained from fasting - then that was good."*[6]

Know, O believer, that if fasting on a journey produces hardship for the servant, then it is not from righteousness, rather it is better and more beloved to Allaah that he breaks his fast. The evidence for this is what has been reported from a number of Companions, *radiyallaahu 'anhum*, that the Prophet (ﷺ) said: *"It is not righteous that you fast on a journey."*[7]

---

3. Reported al-Bukhaaree (4/163) and Muslim (no. 1118).

4. Reported by Ahmad (2/108) and Ibn Hibbaan (no. 2742) from Ibn 'Umar, with *saheeh isnaad*.

5. Reported by Ibn Hibbaan (no. 354), (no. 990) and at-Tabaraanee in *al-Kabeer* (no. 11,881) from Ibn 'Abbaas with a *saheeh isnaad*. Much has been said about the *hadeeth* with its two wordings, but this is not the place to quote it all.

6. Reported by at-Tirmidhee (no. 713) and from him al-Baghawee (no. 1763). Its *isnaad* is *saheeh* even though it contains al-Jurairee - since the narrations of 'Abdul-A'laa from him are some of the most authentic narrations as pointed out by al-'Ijlee and others.

7. Reported by al-Bukhaaree (4/161) and Muslim (no. 1115) from Jaabir.

Some people may think that it is not permissible these days to break the fast on journeys and so they criticise those who accept Allaah's allowance, or others think that it is better to fast due to the ease and availability of means of transport. So we would like to turn their attention to the saying of the One having full knowledge of the unseen and the seen:

"And your Lord is never forgetful."[8]

And His Saying:

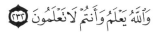

"Allaah knows and you know not."[9]

And His saying in the *Aayah* where he grants the allowance for the traveller to refrain from fasting:

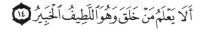

"Allaah intends for you ease, and He does not want to make things difficult for you."[10]

Ease is something which Allaah wishes for the traveller, and it is one of the goals of the magnanimous *Sharee'ah*; and do not forget that the One who laid down the prescriptions of the *Deen* is the Creator of all times, places and people, so He knows better about the peoples' needs and what will improve them and what is fitting for them. He the Mighty and Majestic says:

أَلَا يَعْلَمُ مَنْ خَلَقَ وَهُوَ ٱللَّطِيفُ ٱلْخَبِيرُ ١٤

---

8. Soorah Maryam (19):64

9. Sooratul-Baqarah (2):232

10. Sooratul-Baqarah (2):185

"Should He not know what He created? And He is the Most Kind and Courteous (to His slaves) All-Aware (of everything)."[11]

We quote this so that every Muslim realises that when Allaah and His Messenger have decreed a certain matter then he does not have any choice about it, rather he says along with Allaah's humble believing servants who do not give precedence to anything before Allaah and His Messenger:

$$سَمِعْنَا وَأَطَعْنَا غُفْرَانَكَ رَبَّنَا وَإِلَيْكَ ٱلْمَصِيرُ ۝$$

"We hear, and we obey. (We seek) Your Forgiveness, our Lord, and to You is the return (of all)."[12]

• The ill

Allaah has allowed the sick person to refrain from fasting as mercy for Him, and a convenience. The illness which allows a person to break his fast is that which will, if he fasts, cause him harm, increase in severity, or be prolonged by it - and Allaah knows best.

• Menstruating women and women having post-natal bleeding

There is *ijmaa'* (total consensus) amongst the scholars that menstruating women and women having post-natal bleeding are not allowed to fast and that they must instead refrain from them and make up the days later on. If they fasted that would not count as fasting, and this will be more fully explained later, if Allaah wills.

---

11. Sooratul-Mulk (67):14

12. Sooratul-Baqarah (2):285

• The frail elderly man and woman

Ibn 'Abbaas, *radiyallaahu 'anhumaa,* said: *"The elderly man and old woman who are unable to fast should feed a poor person in place of each day."*[13]

Ad-Daaraqutnee (2/207) reports and declares it authentic by way of Mansoor: from Mujaahid: From Ibn 'Abbaas that he recited:

$$\text{وَعَلَى ٱلَّذِينَ يُطِيقُونَهُۥ فِدْيَةٌ طَعَامُ مِسْكِينٍ}$$

"And as for those who can fast (with difficulty) they have (a choice either fast or) to feed a poor person (for every day)."[14]

and said: *"It is the old man who is unable to fast so he refrains from fasting and instead feeds a poor person with half a saa'*[15] *of wheat."*

Aboo Hurairah, *radiyallaahu 'anhu,* said: *"Whoever reaches old age and is unable to fast the month of Ramadaan, he should give a mudd*[16] *of wheat for each day."*[17]

From Anas ibn Maalik, that one year he became too weak to fast so he prepared a large dish of *thareed*[18] and invited thirty poor people who came and ate their fill.[19]

---

13. Reported by al-Bukhaaree (no. 4505). Refer to *Sharhus-Sunnah* (6/316), *Fathul-Baaree* (8/180), I (4/315) and *Irwaa'-ul-Ghaleel* (4/22-25). Ibn al-Mundhir in his book *al-Ijmaa'* (no. 129) reports that there is *ijmaa'* upon this point.

14. Sooratul-Baqarah (2):184

15. **Translator's note:** The *saa'* is a measure equal to four times the quantity held by the two outstretched hands.

16. **Translator's note:** A *mudd* is the quantity held by the two outstretched hands.

17. Reported by ad-Daaraqutnee (2/208) and its *isnaad* contains 'Abdullaah ibn Saalih who is weak, however it has supports.

18. **Translator's note:** *Thareed:* A broth of crumbled bread and meat.

19. Reported by ad-Daaraqutnee (2/270) and its *isnaad* is *saheeh.*

• The pregnant and breast-feeding women

From Allaah's great Mercy upon His weak servants is that He has allowed some of them to refrain from fasting, and among them are the pregnant women and those who are breast-feeding.

Anas ibn Maalik[20] said: *"A detachment of the cavalry of Allaah's Messenger (ﷺ) attacked us, so I went to Allaah's Messenger(ﷺ) and found him eating, and he said: 'Come and eat.' So I said: 'I am fasting.' He said: 'Come, I shall inform you about the fast - or fasting - indeed, Allaah, the Blessed and Most High, remitted half the prayer for the traveller, and fasting for the pregnant and breast-feeding.' By Allaah the Prophet (ﷺ) said both of these together, or one of them, but how I grieve that I did not eat from the food of the Prophet (ﷺ)."[21]*

---

20. He is (Anas ibn Maalik) al-Ka'bee, not Anas ibn Maalik al-Ansaaree the servant of the Prophet. Rather this was a man from the tribe of 'Abdullaah ibn Ka'b. He settled in Basrah and narrates a single *hadeeth* - this one from the Prophet. See *al-Isaabah* (1/114-115) of Ibn Hajr.

21. Reported by at-Tirmidhee (no. 715), an-Nasaa'ee (4/180), Aboo Daawood (no. 2408) and Ibn Maajah (no. 1667). Its *isnaad* is *hasan* as at-Tirmidhee said.

Chapter 14

Breaking the Fast (*Iftaar*)

• When does the fasting person break his fast?

Allaah, the Most High, says:

$$ثُمَّ أَتِمُّواْ ٱلصِّيَامَ إِلَى ٱلَّيْلِ$$

"Then complete your fast till the nightfall."[1]

Allaah's Messenger (ﷺ) explained this to mean the approach of the night, the passing away of the daylight and the disappearing of the sun below the horizon. We have already quoted enough so that the heart of the Muslim who follows the *Sunnah* will be at rest.

So O servant of Allaah you have the words of Allaah's Messenger (ﷺ) before you and you have read them, his practice is no longer unknown to you, and you have seen the practice of his Companions, *radiyallaahu 'anhum* - and they carefully followed whatever the exemplary Messenger brought.

From 'Amr ibn Maimoon al-Awdee who said: *"The Companions of Muhammad (ﷺ) were the earliest of people in beginning the iftaar and the latest in taking suhoor."*[2]

---

1. Sooratul-Baqarah (2):187

2. Reported by 'Abdur-Razzaaq in *al-Musannaf* (no. 7591) with an *isnaad* declared *saheeh* by al-Haafidh in *al-Fath* (4/199) and al-Haithumee in *Majma' uz-Zawaa'id* (3/154).

• Hastening to break the fast

So brother in *eemaan*, you should break the fast as soon as the sun sets and do not be bothered by the bright redness remaining upon the horizon. In doing this you would be following the *Sunnah* of your Messenger (ﷺ) and differing from the Jews and Christians since they delay breaking the fast until the stars start to appear. Following the way of the Messenger(ﷺ) and applying his *Sunnah* means that the symbols of the *Deen* are raised high, and that we are proud of the guidance which we are upon - and we hope that all souls will gather upon that.

(a) Hastening in breaking the fast brings about good

From Sahl ibn Sa'd, *radiyallaahu 'anhu*, that Allaah's Messenger (ﷺ) said: *"The people will not cease to be upon good as long as they hasten in breaking the fast."*[3]

(b) Hastening in breaking the fast is the *Sunnah* of Allaah's Messenger (ﷺ)

If the Islamic *Ummah* hastens in breaking the fast then it has remained upon the *Sunnah* of the Messenger (ﷺ) and the way of the Pious Predecessors, and they will not go astray, if Allaah wills, as long as they cling firmly to that and reject everything which opposes it.

From Sahl ibn Sa'd, *radiyallaahu 'anhu*, that Allaah's Messenger (ﷺ) said: *"My Ummah will not cease to be upon my Sunnah as long as they do not await the stars when breaking the fast."*[4]

---

3. Reported by al-Bukhaaree (4/173) and Muslim (no. 1093).

4. Reported by Ibn Hibbaan (no. 891) with a *saheeh isnaad*, and its basic meaning is found in the two *Saheehs* as has preceded. The Raafidee Shee'ah are in conformity with the Jews and Christians in their delaying the breaking of the fast until the appearance of the stars - may Allaah save us all from their misguidance.

(c) Hastening to break the fast contrary to those who are misguided and astray, and those upon whom is Allaah's Anger.

If the people continue to be upon good because they follow the way of their Prophet and keep to his *Sunnah* then Islaam will remain uppermost and have the upper hand unharmed by those who oppose it. Then the Muslim *Ummah* will be a lamp shining out through the darkness, and an example to be followed because it will not be a tail for the nations of the east and the west, nor a cover for every shouter of slogans who bends with the wind in whichever direction it takes him.

Aboo Hurairah, *radiyallaahu 'anhu*, said that the Prophet (ﷺ) said: *"The Deen will not cease to be uppermost as long as the people hasten to break the fast, since the Jews and the Christians delay it."*[5]

These *ahaadeeth* contain a number of very important points, which we will explain here:

(i) That the *Deen* remaining uppermost with its banner flying high depends upon acting contrary to those previous nations who were given the Book. There is a lesson in this for the Muslims that they will attain everything good if they remain distinguished upon the guidance - not leaning towards the east or the west; refusing to be a satellite of the Kremlin or to graze upon fodder in the fields of the White House, may Allaah blacken it, and not to turn their faces to London, may Allaah devastate and lay waste to it. Because if they did this (acted contrary to the previous nations) then they would stand out amongst the nations and be looked upon with respect and hearts would have love for them - but that will only happen by returning to the Islaam found in the Book and the *Sunnah*, in *'Aqeedah* (creed) and *Manhaj* (methodology).

---

5. Reported by Aboo Daawood (2/305) and Ibn Hibbaan (no. 224). Its *isnaad* is *hasan*.

(ii) Clinging to Islaam means in its totality and its details, as Allaah the Most High says:

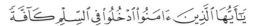

"O you who believe! Enter into Islaam perfectly."[6]

Therefore the division of Islaam into major issues and minor matters is an innovation of modern *jaahiliyyah*[7] and what is intended by it is to confuse the thoughts of the Muslims and to enter them into the whirlpool of concerns which have no basis in the *Deen* of Allaah. In fact their roots extend back to those upon whom is Allaah's Anger, those who believe in a part of the Book and disbelieve in the rest,[8] those whom we have been ordered to act contrary to in general and in specifics, and you are aware that the fruit of acting contrary to the Jews and Christians is that the *Deen* will remain uppermost and strong.

(iii) Calling to Allaah (*ad-Da'wah*) and reminding the believers does not cause disunity. The grave troubles which have beset the Muslim *Ummah* do not make us differentiate between our obligations towards Allaah, nor should they make us prefer some of them over others, treating some so lightly that we end up saying, as many say, 'These are superfluous matters, minor matters, disputed matters, or side issues which we must leave and instead concentrate our efforts on the primary concern which has caused us to disunite!'

O Muslim, who calls to Allaah upon clear proof, you have seen from these *ahaadeeth* that the well being of the *Deen* is dependent upon hastening to break the fast, which depends upon the setting of the sun. So let those people fear Allaah who declare that breaking the fast along with the setting of the sun is discord (*fitnah*) and that calling to revive this *Sunnah* is a call to misguidance and ignorance and takes the Muslims away from their *Deen*. Or that it is a call

---

6. Sooratul-Baqarah (2):208

7. **Publisher's note:** *Jaahiliyyah:* lit. Ignorance. It is also used to describe the pre-Islamic period.

8. **Publisher's note:** See Sooratul-Baqarah (2):85

with no value and that the Muslims cannot possibly be brought to unite upon this since it is a side issue about which there is disagreement, or that it is a minor matter! *And there is no power nor action except by the Will of Allaah.*

(d) Breaking the fast before praying the Maghrib prayer

Allaah's Messenger (ﷺ) used to break the fast before praying.[9] Hastening to break the fast is one of the manners of the Prophets: From Abud-Dardaa', *radiyallaahu 'anhu*: *"Three things are from the manners of the Prophets: hastening in breaking the fast, delaying the suhoor, and placing the right hand upon the left in the Prayer."*[10]

• With what should one break the fast?

Allaah's Messenger (ﷺ) used to encourage the breaking of the fast with dates and if they were not available then with water and this is from the completeness of his (ﷺ) kindness, and concern for his *Ummah* and for giving them sincere advice. The Lord of the worlds, who sent Muhammad as a mercy to them all, says:

$$\text{لَقَدْ جَآءَكُمْ رَسُولٌ مِّنْ أَنفُسِكُمْ عَزِيزٌ عَلَيْهِ مَاعَنِتُّمْ حَرِيصٌ عَلَيْكُم بِٱلْمُؤْمِنِينَ رَءُوفٌ رَّحِيمٌ ۱۲۸}$$

"Verily, there has come unto you a Messenger from amongst yourselves. It grieves him that you should receive any injury or difficulty. He is anxious over you (to be rightly guided, to repent to Allaah, and beg Him to pardon and forgive your sins, in order that you may enter Paradise and be saved from the punishment of the Hell-Fire), for the believers (he is) full of pity, kind, and merciful."[11]

9. Reported by Ahmad (3/163) and Aboo Daawood (no. 2356) from Anas with a *hasan isnaad.*

10. Reported by at-Tabaraanee in *al-Kabeer* as occurs in *al-Majma'* (2/105). Although the narration is *mawqoof* it has the ruling of being *marfoo'.*

11. Sooratut-Tawbah (9): 128

Giving something sweet to an empty stomach leads to its acceptance and that the body takes benefit from it, especially a healthy body which will be strengthened by it. As for water, then the body becomes somewhat dehydrated through fasting and so if it is moistened with water then it can take complete benefit from the food. And know that dates and water contain various blessings and special qualities which have an effect upon the hearts and in purifying them, which will be known only to those who follow (the *Sunnah*).

From Anas, *radiyallaahu 'anhu*, who said: *"The Prophet (ﷺ) used to break the fast with fresh dates before praying, and if not with fresh dates then with older dates, and if not with dates then with some mouthfuls of water."*[12]

• What should a person say when breaking the fast?

O brother, may Allaah guide you and I to follow the *Sunnah* of our Prophet (ﷺ), there is for you a supplication (*du'aa*) which will be answered. So seize this opportunity and call upon Allaah being sure that it will be answered, and know that Allaah does not respond to a heedless and inattentive heart. Call upon Him with supplications for anything good, and hopefully you will attain the good of this life and the Hereafter.

From Aboo Hurairah, *radiyallaahu 'anhu*, who said: He (ﷺ) said: *"Three supplications are answered: the supplication of the fasting person, the supplication of one oppressed and the supplication of the traveller."*[13]

This supplication which will not be rejected, is at the time of breaking the fast as is shown by the *hadeeth* of Aboo Hurairah, *radiallaahu 'anhu*, from the Prophet (ﷺ): *"There are three whose supplications are not rejected: the fasting*

---

12. Reported by Ahmad (3/163), Aboo Daawood (2/306), at-Tirmidhee (3/70) and Ibn Khuzaimah (3/277,278) through two chains from Anas, and its *isnaad* is *saheeh*.

13. Reported by al-'Uqailee in *ad-Du'afaa'* (1/72) and Aboo Muslim al-Kajjee in his *Juz'*. Its *isnaad* is *saheeh* except for the *an'anah* of Yahyaa ibn Abee Katheer, but it has a witness which is the *hadeeth* after it.

person when he breaks his fast, the just ruler and the supplication of the oppressed."[14]

From 'Abdullaah ibn 'Amr ibn al-'Aas who said Allaah's Messenger (ﷺ) said: *"Indeed there is for the fasting person, when he breaks his fast, a supplication which is not rejected."*[15]

Indeed the best *du'aa* is that reported from Allaah's Messenger (ﷺ) and he (ﷺ) used to say when breaking the fast:

$$\text{ذَهَبَ الظَّمَأُ وَٱبْتَلَّتِ ٱلْعُرُوقُ، وَثَبَتَ ٱلْأَجْرُ إِنْ شَاءَ اللهُ}$$

(dhahabadh dhama'u wabtallatil 'urooqu wa thabatal ajru inshaa Allaah)
"The thirst has gone, the veins are moistened and the reward is certain, if Allaah wills."[16]

• Providing food for a fasting person to break his fast

O brother - may Allaah send blessings upon you and enable you to do works of goodness and piety - seek to provide *iftaar* for a fasting person, due to the great reward there is for this. He (ﷺ) said: *"He who gives food for a fasting person to break his fast, he will receive the same reward as him, except that nothing will be reduced from the fasting persons reward."*[17]

---

14. Reported by at-Tirmidhee (no. 2528), Ibn Maajah (no. 1752) and Ibn Hibbaan (no. 2407). Its *isnaad* contains Aboo Mudillah who is unknown.

15. Reported by Ibn Maajah (1/557), al-Haakim (1/422), Ibn as-Sunnee (no. 128) and at-Tayaalisee (no. 299) through two chains of narration from him and al-Boosairee said: (2/81): *This isnaad is saheeh, its narrators are reliable.*

16. Reported by Aboo Daawood (2/306), al-Baihaqee (4/239), al-Haakim (1/422), Ibn Sunnee, an-Nasaa'ee in *Amalul-Yawm* (269) and Daraqutnee who declared its *isnaad* to be *hasan*, and it is as he said.

17. Reported by Ahmad (4/114-6 and 5/192), at-Tirmidhee (no. 804), Ibn Maajah (no. 1746) and Ibn Hibbaan (no. 895). At-Tirmdhee declared it *saheeh* and it is as he said.

If a Muslim who is fasting is invited by someone then he must accept the invitation, since anyone who does not respond to the invitation has disobeyed Abul-Qaasim (ﷺ), and he should be certain that the acceptance will not reduce any of his good deeds or reduce his reward. It is also recommended for the guest to supplicate for the host, after finishing the food, with one of the supplications reported from the Prophet (ﷺ) such as his (ﷺ) saying:

(a) أَكَلَ طَعَامَكُمُ الْأَبْرَارُ، وَصَلَّتْ عَلَيْكُمُ ٱلْمَلَائِكَةُ، وَأَفْطَرَ عِنْدَكُمُ الصَّائِمُونَ

(Akala ta'aamakumul abraaru, wasallat 'alaykumul malaa'ikatu, wa aftara 'indakumus saa'imoon)

"May the righteous eat along with you, the angels seek forgiveness for you, and those who fast, break their fast along with you."[18]

(b) اللّٰهُمَّ أَطْعِمْ مَنْ أَطْعَمَنِي، وَاسْقِ مَنْ سَقَانِي

(Allaahumma at'im man at'amanee, wasqi man saqaanee)

"O Allaah feed the one who fed me, and give drink to the one who gave me drink."[19]

(c) اللّٰهُمَّ اغْفِرْ لَهُمْ وَارْحَمْهُمْ وَبَارِكْ فِيمَا رَزَقْتَهُمْ

(Allaahum maghfirlahum warhamhum wa baarik feemaa razaqtahum)

"O Allaah forgive them, and have mercy upon them and place blessing in what you have provided for them."[20]

---

18. Reported by Ibn Abee Shaibah (3/100), Ahmad (3/118), an-Nasaa'ee in *'Amalul Yawm* (no. 268), Ibn as-Sunnee (no. 129) and 'Abdur-Razzaaq (4/311) through various chains. Its *isnaad* is *saheeh*. Note: The addition which some people give to this *hadeeth*: *Wa dhakarakumullaahu fee man 'indahu* (and may Allaah make mention of you to those near Him) - then it has no basis here at all so be aware.

19. Reported by Muslim (no. 2055) from al-Miqdaad.

20. Reported by Muslim (no. 2042) from 'Abdullaah ibn Busr.

Chapter 15

Actions Which Nullify the Fast

There are many things which a fasting person must avoid since if he commits them during the day in Ramadaan his fast will be broken and thus be added to his sins, and they are:

• Eating and drinking deliberately

Allaah, the Most Mighty says:

وَكُلُوا۟ وَٱشْرَبُوا۟ حَتَّىٰ يَتَبَيَّنَ لَكُمُ ٱلْخَيْطُ ٱلْأَبْيَضُ مِنَ ٱلْخَيْطِ ٱلْأَسْوَدِ مِنَ ٱلْفَجْرِ ۖ ثُمَّ أَتِمُّوا۟ ٱلصِّيَامَ إِلَى ٱلَّيْلِ ۚ

"And eat and drink until the white thread (light) of dawn appears to you distinct from the black thread (darkness of night), then complete your fast till the nightfall."[1]

Therefore it is known that fasting is abstaining from eating and drinking, so if the fasting person eats or drinks then he has broken his fast. This applies only to the one who does so consciously, and not to the one who does it forgetfully or accidentally, or is forced to do it. This is known by the following proofs:

---

1. Sooratul-Baqarah (2):187

64

He (ﷺ) said: *"If one of you eats and drinks out of forgetfulness, then let him complete his fast, for it was indeed Allaah who gave him food and drink."[2]*

He (ﷺ) said: *"Allaah has excused for my Ummah mistakes, forgetfulness and what they are forced to do."[3]*

• Making oneself vomit

One who has an attack of vomiting there is nothing upon him; he (ﷺ) said: *"Whoever has an attack of vomiting, then no atonement is required of him, but whoever vomits intentionally then let him make atonement[4] for it."[5]*

• Menstruation and after-birth bleeding

When a woman begins to menstruate or begins after-birth bleeding during the day in Ramadaan, whether it is at the start or the end of the day then her fast is broken and she must make up by fasting another day in place of it, and if she were to continue fasting it would not count.

He (ﷺ) said: *"Is it not that if she menstruates then she does not pray, nor fast?"* We said: *"Yes indeed."* He said: *"Then that is the deficiency in her Deen."* And in a narration: *"She remains not praying at night and refraining from fasting in Ramadaan then that is the deficiency in her Deen."[6]*

---

2. Reported by al-Bukhaaree (4/135) and Muslim (no. 1155).

3. Reported by at-Tahaawee in *Sharh Ma'aanee ul-Aathaar* (2/56), al-Haakim (2/198), Ibn Hazm in *al-Ihkaam* (5/149) and ad-Daaraqutnee (4/171) from Ibn 'Abbaas and its *isnaad* is *saheeh*.

4. **Translator's note:** Meaning fast another day in its place.

5. Reported by Aboo Daawood (2/310), at-Tirmidhee (3/79), Ibn Maajah (1/536) and Ahmad (2/498) from Aboo Hurairah. Its *isnaad* is *saheeh* as Shaikhul-Islaam Ibn Taimiyyah said in *Haqeeqatus-Siyaam* (p. 14).

6. Reported by Muslim (no. 79 and 80) from Ibn 'Umar and Aboo Hurairah.

The order to make up for it by fasting other days is reported in the *hadeeth* of Mu'aadhah who said: *I asked 'Aa'ishah saying: "Why is it that the menstruating woman has to make up her fasts but not the Prayers?" She said: "Are you a Harooree[7] woman?!" I said: "I am not a Harooree woman, but I wish to ask." She said: "That used to come upon us and so we were ordered to make up the fasts and were never ordered to make up the prayers."[8]*

• Injections containing nourishment

This is giving nourishment intravenously so that it reaches the intestines, with the intention of nourishing a sick person. This breaks the fast since it involves entering nourishment into the stomach.[9]

Also if the injection does not reach the intestines but reaches the blood-stream then it likewise breaks the fast since it is being used in place of food and drink. It often happens that sick people in a coma for a long while are fed with the like of those drips containing glucose and saline solution and the same goes for the inhalers which those who suffer from asthma use - they also break the fast .

• Sexual intercourse

Ash-Shawkaanee said in *ad-Daraariyyul-Mudiyyah* (2/22): "There is no disagree-ment that sexual intercourse breaks the fast if it is done deliberately, however

---

7. The *Haroorees*: Referring to the land of Harooraa a town two miles away from Koofah. One who holds the beliefs of the Khawaarij is called Harooree, since the first of them to appear rebelled against 'Alee, *radiyallaahu 'anhu*, and stayed at that place as pointed out by Ibn Hajr in *Fathul-Baree* (4/424) also see *al-Lubaab* of Ibn al-Atheer (1/359). These Haroorees make it obligatory upon the woman that when she becomes clean of her menses she must make up the prayers she missed. So 'Aa'ishah, *radiyallaahu 'anhaa*, feared that Mu'aadhah had learnt her question from the Khawaarij whose habit was to oppose the *Sunnah* with their own opinion and analogy - and their like in our time are many! Refer to the chapter *at-Tawtheeq 'anillaah wa Rasoolihi* of Saleem al-Hilaalee's treatise: *Diraasaat Manhajiyyah fil 'Aqeedatis-Salafiyyah*.

8. Reported by al-Bukhaaree (4/429) and Muslim (no. 335).

9. See *Haqeeqatus-Siyaam* of Ibn Taimiyyah (p. 55).

66

if it is done by one due to forgetfulness then some scholars make it the same as one who eats or drinks forgetfully."

Ibn al-Qayyim said in *Zaadul-Ma'aad* (2/60): "The Qur'aan shows that sexual intercourse breaks the fast, just like eating and drinking - no disagreement is known concerning this."

The proof of this from the Book of Allaah the Mighty and Majestic is:

$$\text{فَٱلْـَٔنَ بَـٰشِرُوهُنَّ وَٱبْتَغُوا۟ مَا كَتَبَ ٱللَّهُ لَكُمْ}$$

"So now have sexual relations with them and seek that which Allaah has ordained for you (i.e. offspring)."[10]

So Allaah allowed *mubaasharah* (meaning sexual intercourse), so it is known from this that fasting is withholding from sexual intercourse, eating and drinking. So whoever nullifies his fast with sexual intercourse then he must make up the fast with another day (*qadaa*) and also give expiation (*kaffaarah*) for that, and the proof for this is the narration of Aboo Hurairah, *radiyallaahu 'anhu*, from the Prophet (ﷺ): *That a man came to him and said: "O Messenger of Allaah I am destroyed." He asked: "What has destroyed you?" He said: "I cohabited with my wife in Ramadaan." He asked: "Are you able to free a slave?" He replied: "No." He asked: "Are you able to fast two months consecutively?" He replied: "No." He asked: "Are you able to feed sixty poor people?" He replied: "No." He said: "Then sit." So he sat down. Then a large basket of palm leaves containing dates was brought to the Prophet (ﷺ) and he said: "Give this in charity." He said: "There is no one between its two lava-plains poorer than us." So the Prophet (ﷺ) smiled until his molar teeth became visible and said: "Take it and feed it to your family."*[11]

---

10. Sooratul-Baqarah (2):187

11. The *hadeeth* is established with various wordings. Reported by al-Bukhaaree (11/516), Muslim (no. 1111) Aboo Dawood (no. 2390), at-Tirmidhee (no. 724), Ibn Maajah (no. 1671) and others. Some report it in *mursal* form and others in connected form. Some of them declare the addition *"And fast a day in its place"* to be authentic, this is declared *saheeh* by al-Haafidh Ibn Hajr in *al-Fath* (11/516) and it is as he said.

Chapter 16

Atonement (*al-Qadaa*)

1. Know, O Muslim - may Allaah grant us and you knowledge of His *Deen* - that it is not obligatory to make up the missed days from Ramadaan immediately afterwards, rather it is an obligation which may be delayed, due to what is reported from 'Aa'ishah, *radiyallaahu 'anhaa*: "*It used to be that I had days to make up for Ramadaan and I would not be able to do so except in Sha'baan.*"[1]

Al-Haafidh, *rahimahullaah*, says in *al-Fath* (4/191): "the *hadeeth* contains a proof of the allowance of delaying making up missed Ramadaan fasts unrestrictedly whether due to excuse or not."

Although, obviously it is better to hasten in making up the fasts than to delay them, since this falls under the general proofs concerning hastening to do good works and not delaying them - and the proof from the Noble Book is:

وَسَارِعُوٓاْ إِلَىٰ مَغۡفِرَةٖ مِّن رَّبِّكُمۡ

"And be quick in the race for forgiveness from your Lord."[2]

---

1. Reported by al-Bukhaaree (4/166) and Muslim (no. 1146).
Translator's note: Sha'baan being the eighth month, immediately preceding Ramadaan.

2. Soorah Aal-'Imraan (3):133.

and the saying of the Mighty and Majestic:

$$\text{أُوْلَـٰٓئِكَ يُسَـٰرِعُونَ فِى ٱلْخَيْرَٰتِ وَهُمْ لَهَا سَـٰبِقُونَ} \ (٦١)$$

"It is those who race for the good deeds, and they are foremost in them."[3]

2. It is not obligatory to make up the days together (i.e. one immediately after the other) as it was obligatory to fast initially, as Allaah the Most High says:

$$\text{فَعِدَّةٌ مِّنْ أَيَّامٍ أُخَرَ}$$

"The same number (of days which one did not fast must be made up) from other days."[4]

Ibn 'Abbaas said: *"There is no harm if he fasts them separately."*[5]

Aboo Hurairah, *radiyallaahu 'anhu*, said: *"He may fast them together if he wishes."*[6]

Al-Baihaqee (4/259) and ad-Daaraqutnee (2/191-192) report by way of 'Abdur-Rahmaan ibn Ibraaheem: from al-'Alaa ibn 'Abdir-Rahmaan: from his father: from Aboo Hurairah in *marfoo'* form: *"Whoever has the fasts of Ramadaan to make up then let him fast them one after the other without interruption."*

However this *hadeeth* is weak (*da'eef*). Ad-Daaraqutnee says: "'Abdur-Rahmaan ibn Ibraaheem is weak." Al-Baihaqee says: "He is declared weak by Ibn Ma'een, an-Nasaa'ee and ad-Daaraqutnee." Ibn Hajr reports in at-

---

3. Sooratul-Mu'minoon (23):61

4. Sooratul-Baqarah (2):185

5. Reported in *mu'allaq* form by al-Bukhaaree (4/189) and connected by 'Abdur Razzaaq, ad-Daaraqutnee and Ibn Abee Shaibah with *saheeh isnaad*. See *Taghleequt-Ta'leeq* (3/186).

6. Reported by ad-Daaraqutnee and it is *saheeh*. See *al-Irwaa'* (4/95).

Talkheesul-Habeer (6/206) from Ibn Abee Haatim that he criticised this *hadeeth* of 'Abdur-Rahmaan in particular. Our Shaikh al-Albaanee, has fully explained its weakness in *al-Irwaa'* (no. 943), that which he has written in *Silsilatul-Ahaadeeth ad-Da'eefah* (2/137) which indicates that this *hadeeth* is *hasan* has been retracted by him,[7] so be aware.

In conclusion, there is no *hadeeth,* as far as we know, from the Prophet (ﷺ) referring to fasting the missed days together or separately, so what is clearest, easiest and most convenient is that both are allowed, and this is the saying of the Imaam of *Ahlus-Sunnah* Ahmad ibn Hanbal, *rahimahullaah.* Aboo Daawood says in his *Masaa'il* (p. 95): "I heard Ahmad being asked about making up the missed fasts of Ramadaan, so he said: 'If he wishes he may split them up and if he wishes he may fast them together.'" And Allaah knows best. However, the permissibility of separating them does not mean a denial of fasting them together.

3) All the scholars are united that one who dies and has missed a number of obligatory prayers then neither his heir nor anyone else can pray them on his behalf. The same goes for one who is unable to fast, no one can fast on his behalf whilst he is alive, rather he should feed a poor person for each day as Anas, *radiyallaahu 'anhu*, did in the narration we have already quoted (see p.54). However one who dies and has not fasted a fast which he vowed (*nadhr*) to keep, then in this case his heir should fast it on his behalf due to his (ﷺ) saying: *"Whoever dies and there is a fast remaining obligatory upon him - then his heir should fast for him."*[8]

---

7. We have fully clarified this by asking our Shaikh verbally and he - may Allaah benefit the people by him - mentioned the like of what we have written here, so all praise is for Allaah as befits Him.

8. Reported by al-Bukhaaree (4/168) and Muslim (no. 1147) from 'Aa'ishah *radiyallaahu 'anhaa.*

From Ibn 'Abbaas, *radiyallaahu 'anhumaa*, who said: "*A man came to the Prophet (ﷺ) and said: 'O Messenger of Allaah my mother has died and a month of fasting is obligatory upon her, shall I make it up for her?' He said: 'Yes for the debt to Allaah has more right to be settled.'*"⁹

These *ahaadeeth* are general and indicate the prescription of the heirs making up any kind of fast for the deceased, and this is the view of some of the Shaafi'ees and of Ibn Hazm (*al-Muhallaa*, 7/28). However, these *ahaadeeth* are examples of general *ahaadeeth* which have been particularised to the case of a fast made obligatory through a vow. This is the saying of Imaam Ahmad as occurs in *Masaa'ilul-Imaam Ahmad* of Aboo Daawood (p. 96) who said: "I heard Ahmad ibn Hanbal say: 'One should not fast on behalf of the deceased except what is due because of a vow.' Aboo Daawood said: 'I said to Ahmad: Then what about the month of Ramadaan?' He said: 'He should give food on his behalf.'"

This is the opinion that one feels most comfortable and satisfied with due to the evidences - since it means that all the *ahaadeeth* are acted upon without rejecting any of them, and furthermore correctly understanding them which is particularly seen regarding the first of them - since 'Aa'ishah, *radiyallaahu 'anhaa*, did not understand it to refer unrestrictedly to include even the fast of Ramadaan and other fasts, rather she held that in such cases one should feed the poor on their behalf.

This is also shown by what is reported from 'Amrah; that her mother died and some days remained obligatory upon her from Ramadaan, so she said to 'Aa'ishah: "*Shall I fast them on her behalf?*" she said: "*No, rather give charity on her behalf of half a saa' for each poor person for each day.*" ¹⁰

---

9. Reported by al-Bukhaaree (4/169) and Muslim (no. 1148).

10. Reported by at-Tahaawee in *Mushkilul-Aathaar* (3/142) and Ibn Hazm in *al-Muhallaa* (7/4) and the wording is his. Its *isnaad* is *saheeh*.

As is established that the narrator of a *hadeeth* knows best its meaning: the Scholar of this *Ummah* [Ibn 'Abbaas] *radiyallaahu 'anhumaa,* is also of this opinion as is shown by his saying: *"If a man becomes ill in Ramadaan and dies having refrained from fasting, then food should be given on his behalf and no making up of the days is due, and if a fast due to a vow was obligatory upon him, then his heir should fast on his behalf."* [11]

As is known Ibn 'Abbaas, *radiyallaahu anhumaa,* is the narrator of the second *hadeeth* and particularly since he reports a *hadeeth* clearly showing that the heir should fast on behalf of the dead if it is a fast he vowed to make: *"That Sa'ad ibn Ubaadah, radiyallaahu 'anhu, asked Allaah's Messenger (ﷺ) saying: 'My mother has died and had vowed [to fast].' He said: 'Make it up for her.'"* [12]

This distinction (between the fasts of Ramadaan and a fast due to a vow) is fully in keeping with the principles of the *Sharee'ah* as explained by Ibn al-Qayyim in *I'laamul-Muwaqqi'een* and he further clarifies the matter in *Tahdheeb Abee Daawood* (3/279-282) - so refer to it for it is important.

4) If a person dies and an obligatory fast due to a vow was upon him, then if the same number of people as the days due, fast on his behalf, then that is permissible. Al-Hasan said: *"If thirty people fast on his behalf, each of them a single day then it is allowed."* [13]

The heir may gather a number of poor people, equal to the number of missed fasts, and feed them; this is permissible since it was done by Anas ibn Maalik, *radiyallaahu 'anhu.*

---

11. Reported by Aboo Daawood with *saheeh isnaad* and by Ibn Hazm in *al-Muhallaa* (7/7) who declared its *isnaad* to be *saheeh.*

12. Reported by al-Bukhaaree, Muslim and others.

13. Reported by al-Bukhaaree in *mu'allaq* form (4/112) and it is connected by ad-Daaraqutnee in *Kitaabul-Mudabbaj.* Our Shaikh al-Albaanee declares that its *isnaad* is *saheeh* in *Mukhtasar Saheehil-Bukhaaree* (1/58). Also see *Taghleequt Ta'leeq* (3/189).

Chapter 17

Expiation (*al-Kaffaarah*)

(1) The *hadeeth* of Aboo Hurairah, *radiyallaahu 'anhu,* about the man who cohabited with his wife in Ramadaan has preceded[1] and that he had to make up the day and also give expiation, which is freeing a slave, and if he is not able to then to fast two months consecutively, and if he is not able to then to feed sixty poor people.

It is said that the expiation for sexual intercourse is to choose one of the three, not that he has to necessarily do the first, if he is unable then the second, and if he is unable to do even that, then the third.

However, those who report this order are greater in number and so their narration is stronger. Furthermore, their narration contains an additional piece of knowledge, since they agree that the fast was broken due to sexual intercourse, and this is not reported in the other narrations and whoever knows something, is a proof over and above one who does not. The view that the order must be adhered to is also supported by the fact that it is safer since by acting upon it ones expiation will definitely be acceptable even if we hold that one has a choice - as opposed to the opposite case.

(2) One who has to make expiation but is unable to free a slave, fast two months, or to feed the poor - then it is not binding upon him since something

---

1. For the full text of *hadeeth* refer to p. 67.

is only required when one is able to do it. Allaah the Most High says:

$$\text{لَا يُكَلِّفُ ٱللَّهُ نَفْسًا إِلَّا وُسْعَهَا}$$

"Allaah burdens not a person beyond his scope."[2]

This is shown by the action of the Prophet (ﷺ) since he discharged the man from the expiation when he informed him that he was unable and he gave him a basket of dates to feed his family with.

(3) Expiation was not binding upon the woman, since the Prophet (ﷺ) was informed of an action which took place between the man and his wife, but the Messenger (ﷺ) made only a single expiation obligatory, and Allaah knows best.

---

2. Sooratul-Baqarah (2):286.

Chapter 18

Recompense (al-Fidyah)

1. The pregnant and breast feeding women who fear for themselves or their children, should refrain from fasting and instead feed a poor person for each day, the proof for this is from the Book of Allaah:

وَعَلَى ٱلَّذِينَ يُطِيقُونَهُۥ فِدْيَةٌ طَعَامُ مِسْكِينٍ

"And as for those who can fast (with difficulty) they have (a choice either to fast or) to feed a poor person (for every day)."[1]

This *Aayah* is a proof here since it is particular to the old man and old woman, the sick person who remains continually in that state and the pregnant and breast feeding women who fear for themselves or their children as will be shown from Ibn 'Abbaas and Ibn 'Umar, *radiyallaahu 'anhum*.

2. You have come to know O brother in *Eemaan*, from what has preceded, that this *Aayah* was abrogated as shown by the *hadeeth* of 'Abdullaah ibn 'Umar and that of Salamah ibn al-Akwa'[2], *radiyallaahu 'anhum*, except that it is established that Ibn 'Abbaas said that it is not abrogated[3] but that it refers to the old man and the old woman who are unable to fast and so instead should

---

1. Sooratul-Baqarah (2):184.

2. See p.15.

3. See p.54.

feed a poor person for each day.[4]

So it may be thought that Ibn 'Abbaas is in contradiction with the majority of the Companions and contradicting himself - particularly when you know that he clearly states that it was abrogated in a different narration: *"Allowance was made for the old man and the old woman, who were both able to fast that they could fast if they wished, or instead feed a poor person for every day and they did not have to make up the days - then that was abrogated in this Aayah:*

فَمَن شَهِدَ مِنكُمُ ٱلشَّهْرَ فَلْيَصُمْهُ

"So whoever of you sights (the crescent on the first night of) the month (of Ramadaan), he must fast that month."[5]

And that was affirmed for the old man and old woman who were unable to fast, and the pregnant and breast feeding women who feared that they should refrain from fasting, but feed a poor person for each day."[6]

Some people look at the apparent meaning of the previous narration reported by al-Bukhaaree in the *Book of Tafseer* of his *Saheeh* which clearly denies abrogation and they think that the *Scholar of the Ummah* (i.e. Ibn 'Abbaas) is contradicting the majority of the Companions. When they are struck by the narration clearly stating abrogation they claim that this is a contradiction!

3. The truth, about which there is no doubt, is that the *Aayah* is abrogated (*mansookh*). However, abrogated in the sense understood by the early generations. The Pious Predecessors used *abrogation* to apply to cases where a general, unrestricted or apparent meaning was later particularised, re-stricted or explained, to the extent that they would even describe exceptions

---

4. Reported by al-Bukhaaree (8/135).

5. Sooratul-Baqarah (2):185.

6. Reported by Ibn al-Jarood (no. 381), al-Baihaqee (4/230) and Aboo Daawood (no. 2315). Its *isnaad* is *saheeh*.

made, conditions and further descriptions as being abrogation (*naskh*) - since these involve removal of what is apparent and explanation of what is actually meant. Thus abrogation in their usage was explanation of what is meant - not by that wording itself, but by a different text.[7]

If anyone considers their words he will find examples of this so plentiful that they cannot be enumerated and any difficulty passes away which is caused by taking their words and applying modern definitions to them - i.e. that the definition of *abrogation* is: "Removal of a previous *Sharee'ah* ruling by a *Sharee'ah* text that came later - as far as those legally obliged are concerned."

4. What we have stated is supported by the fact that the *Aayah* is general covering everyone legally obliged. It covers those who are able to fast and those who are unable, and the witness for it is in the *Sunnah*. Imaam Muslim reports from Salamah ibn al-Akwa' *radiyallaahu 'anhu*, who said: "*In Ramadaan in the time of the Messenger of Allaah (ﷺ) it used to be the case that whoever wished fasted, and whoever wished refrained and instead fed a poor person until this Aayah was sent down:*

$$فَمَن شَهِدَ مِنكُمُ ٱلشَّهْرَ فَلْيَصُمْهُ$$

"So whoever of you sights (the crescent on the first night of) the month (of Ramadaan) he must fast that month."[8]

Perhaps the problem in understanding the *hadeeth* of Ibn 'Abbaas which clearly states that there was abrogation is that the allowance used to be for the old man and the old woman - who were able to fast. However the misunderstanding disappears when it becomes clear that this is an example, not that they were the only ones who had the allowance. The proof for this understanding is the *hadeeth* itself, since if the allowance was only for the old man and old woman, then it was abrogated and still remained an allowance

---

7. Refer to: *I'laamul-Muwaqqi'een* (1/35) of Ibn al-Qayyim and *al-Muwaafiqaat* (3/118) of ash-Shaatibee.

8. Sooratul-Baqarah (2):185.

for them, then what is this allowance which has been affirmed and denied if they are the only cases rather than being mentioned as examples? So if this is clear to you then you will be sure that the meaning of the *Aayah* has been abrogated with regard to those who are able to fast, but not abrogated with regard to those who are unable to fast. The first ruling is established to have been abrogated as shown by the Qur'aan, but the second ruling remains as shown by the *Sunnah* and will not be abrogated until the Day of Resurrection.

This is further supported by what Ibn 'Abbaas says in the narration affirming abrogation: *"It remains for the old man and the old woman who cannot fast and for the pregnant and breast feeding women if they fear - they should refrain from fasting and instead feed a poor person for each day."*

It is made even clearer by the *hadeeth* of Mu'aadh ibn Jabal, *radiyallaahu 'anhu*, who said: *"As regards to stages of fasting - then Allaah's Messenger (ﷺ) came to al-Madeenah and fasted three days from every month, and the fast of 'Aashooraa. Then Allaah obligated fasting and sent down:*

$$كُتِبَ عَلَيْكُمُ ٱلصِّيَامُ كَمَا كُتِبَ عَلَى ٱلَّذِينَ مِن قَبْلِكُمْ لَعَلَّكُمْ تَتَّقُونَ ۝$$

"...Fasting is prescribed for you as it was prescribed for those before you, that you may become pious"[9] *Then Allaah sent down the other Aayah:*

$$شَهْرُ رَمَضَانَ ٱلَّذِىٓ أُنزِلَ فِيهِ ٱلْقُرْءَانُ$$

"The month of Ramadaan in which was revealed the Qur'aan..."[10] *So Allaah obligated the fast upon the healthy resident, and made allowance for the sick and the traveller, and He obligated feeding [a poor person] upon the old man unable to fast - so these are the two stages..."*[11]

---

9. Sooratul-Baqarah (2):183.

10. Sooratul-Baqarah (2):185.

11. Reported by Aboo Daawood (no. 507), al-Baihaqee (4/200) and Ahmad (5/246-247). Its *isnaad* is *saheeh*.

So these two *ahaadeeth* clearly show that the *Aayah* was abrogated with regard to the one who is able to fast, but not abrogated with regard to one unable to fast. In other words the *Aayah* was made particular. Therefore Ibn 'Abbaas is in agreement with the other Companions, and his *hadeeth* is in agreement with that of 'Abdullaah ibn 'Umar and that of Salamah ibn al-Akwa', *radiyallaahu anhum*. Likewise his sayings do not contradict one another since his saying: *It was not abrogated* is explained by his saying: *It was abrogated* - meaning: The *Aayah* was made particular. Thus it becomes clear that abrogation in the understanding of the Companions is the same as particularisation and restriction to the later scholars of the *Principles of Fiqh* - and this is something indicated by al-Qurtubee in his *Tafseer* (2/288).

5. Perhaps you may think, O Muslim, that what is established from Ibn 'Abbaas and Mu'aadh, *radiyallaahu 'anhumaa*, was just their opinion, or judgment, and cannot therefore rise to the level of a prophetic *hadeeth* which can abrogate the Qur'aan, restrict its unrestricted matters, and explain details. The answer to these doubts is as follows:

(a) That these two *ahaadeeth* have the ruling of being *marfoo'* [i.e. of being traced back to the Prophet (ﷺ)] by agreement of the scholars of the *ahaadeeth* of Allaah's Messenger (ﷺ). So it is not permissible for a Believer who loves Allaah and His Messenger to oppose them when they are established with him, since they are giving an explanation connected with the reason for the revelation of an *Aayah*, meaning: these two Companions who were present when revelation was descending are informing us that a certain *Aayah* from the Qur'aan was revealed concerning something particular. Thus this is a *hadeeth* which is therefore traced back to the Prophet (ﷺ) without a doubt.[12]

(b) Ibn 'Abbaas affirmed this ruling for the pregnant and the breast feeding woman. Where did he take this ruling from? There is no doubt that it was

---

12. Refer to: *Tadreebur-Raawee* (1/192-193) of as-Suyootee and *Uloomul-Hadeeth* (p. 24) of Ibn as-Salaah.

taken from the *Sunnah*, particularly since he is not alone in that, rather 'Abdullaah ibn 'Umar, who reports that this *Aayah* was abrogated, agrees with him.

From Maalik: from Naafi': from Ibn 'Umar: *That he was asked about a pregnant woman who feared for her child, so he said: "She should refrain from fasting and she should feed a mudd[13] of wheat to a poor person in place of every day."*[14]

Ad-Daaraqutnee reports (1/207) from Ibn 'Umar, and he declares it *saheeh*, that he said: *"The pregnant woman and the breast-feeding woman should break the fast and not make up the days."* He reports it through another chain: *"that a pregnant woman asked him, so he said: 'Refrain from fasting, but feed a poor person for every day and do not make up the fasts.'"* Its *isnaad* is good. And through a third chain from him: *"That a daughter of his was married to a man of the Quraish and she was pregnant and she became very thirsty in Ramadaan so he ordered her to break the fast and to feed a poor person for every day."*

(c) That none of the Companions disagreed with Ibn 'Abbaas.[15]

6. This explains what is meant by the exemption from fasting for the pregnant and breast-feeding woman which occurs in the previous *hadeeth* of Anas ibn Maalik al-Ka'bee. It is restricted to refer to one who fears for herself or her child, and that she has to make recompense, but not make up the fasts. Ad-Daaraqutnee reports with an *isnaad* which he declares *saheeh* (1/207) from Ibn 'Abbaas that he saw a slave-girl of his, pregnant or breast-feeding, so he said: *"You are one of those who are unable, upon you is recompense and there is no atonement (qadaa) due upon you."*

---

13. See Glossary for the meaning of *Mudd*.

14. Reported by al-Baihaqee (4/230) by way of Imaam ash-Shaafi'ee and its *isnaad* is *saheeh*.

15. As stated by Ibn Qudaamah in *al-Mughnee* (3/21).

7. Whoever thinks that the exemption from fasting for the pregnant and breast-feeding woman is the same as that for the traveller and that therefore she has to make up the missed fasts (qadaa), then his saying is rejected since the Qur'aan explains the meaning of the exemption from fasting for the traveller:

$$فَمَن كَانَ مِنكُم مَّرِيضًا أَوْ عَلَىٰ سَفَرٍ فَعِدَّةٌ مِّنْ أَيَّامٍ أُخَرَ$$

"If any of you is ill or on a journey, the same number (should be made up) from other days."[16]

Likewise He explained what is meant by the exemption from fasting for the one who is unable :

$$وَعَلَى ٱلَّذِينَ يُطِيقُونَهُ فِدْيَةٌ طَعَامُ مِسْكِينٍ$$

"And as for those who can fast (with difficulty), they have (a choice either to fast or) to feed a poor person (for every day)."[17]

It has been established that the pregnant and breast-feeding women are encompassed by this *Aayah* - indeed it refers to them in particular.

---

16. Sooratul-Baqarah (2):184.

17. Sooratul-Baqarah (2):184.

Chapter 19

Lailatul-Qadr (The Night of Decree)

Its excellence is great, since in this night the Noble Qur'aan was sent down, which leads one who clings to it, to the path of honour and nobility, and raises him to the summit of distinction and everlasting life. The Muslims who adhere strictly to the *Sunnah* of Allaah's Messenger (ﷺ) do not raise flags on this night, nor suspend colourful decorations. Rather they vie in standing during it (*Lailatul-Qadr*) in Prayer out of sincere faith and hoping for reward. Here, O Muslim, are the Quranic *Aayaat* and authentic prophetic *ahaadeeth* referring to this night:

• Its excellence

As regards its excellence it is more than sufficient to mention that *Lailatul-Qadr* is better than a thousand months, He, the Mighty and Majestic, says:

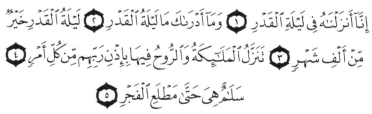

"**Verily! We have sent it (this Qur'aan) down in the Night of Decree (*Lailatul-Qadr*). And what will make you know what the Night of Decree is? The Night of Decree is better than a thousand months. Therein descend the angels and the *Rooh* (ie. Gabriel) by Allaah's**

Permission with all Decrees, Peace! until the appearance of dawn." [1]

And in it every decreed matter for the year is conveyed, He, the Most High says:

"**We sent it (this Qur'aan) down on a blessed Night. Verily, We are ever warning (mankind of Our Torment). Therein (that Night) is decreed every matter of ordainment.** *Amran* **(i.e. a command or this Qur'aan or His Decree of every matter) from Us. Verily, We are ever sending (the Messenger). (As) a Mercy from your Lord. Verily! He is the All-Hearer, the All-Knower."** [2]

• When is it?

It is reported from the Prophet (ﷺ) that it is within the twenty first, twenty-third, twenty-fifth, twenty-seventh, twenty-ninth or the last night of Ramadaan. [3]

Imaam ash-Shaafi'ee, *rahimahullaah*, said: *To me it is as the Prophet(ﷺ) used to answer according to the question posed, it would be said to him: "Shall I seek it in such and such night?" So he would reply: "Seek it in such and such night." And Allaah knows best.* [4]

The most correct saying is that it occurs in the odd nights of the last ten nights of Ramadaan and this is shown by the *hadeeth* of 'Aa'ishah, *radiyallaahu 'anhaa,*

---

1. Sooratul-Qadr (97):1-5.

2. Sooratud-Dukhaan (44):3-6.

3. There are many different sayings about it, Imaam al-'Iraaqee has written a treatise on this entitled *Sharhus-Sadr Fee Dhikr Lailatul-Qadr* in which he gathers the sayings of the scholars.

4. Reported from him by al-Baghawee in *Sharhus-Sunnah* (6/388).

who said: *"Allaah's Messenger (ﷺ) used to practice i'tikaaf in the last ten nights and say: 'Seek out Lailatul-Qadr in the (odd nights) of the last ten of Ramadaan.'"*[5]

However if the servant is too weak or unable, then he should at least not let the last seven pass him by, due to what is reported from Ibn 'Umar, who said: Allaah's Messenger (ﷺ) said: *"Seek it in the last ten, and if one of you is too weak or unable then let him not allow that to make him miss the final seven."*[6]

This explains his (ﷺ) saying: *"I see that your dreams are in agreement (that it is in the last seven) so he who wishes to seek it out then let him seek it in the last seven."*[7]

It is known from the *Sunnah,* that knowledge of the exact night upon which *Lailatul-Qadr* falls was taken up because the people argued, 'Ubaadah ibn as-Saamit, *radiyallaahu 'anhu,* said: The Prophet (ﷺ) *came out intending to tell us about Lailatul-Qadr, however two men were arguing and he said: "I came out to inform you about Lailatul-Qadr but so and so, and, so and so were arguing, so it was raised up, and perhaps that is better for you, so seek it on the (twenty) ninth and the (twenty) seventh and the (twenty) fifth."*[8]

Some of the *ahaadeeth* indicate that *Lailatul-Qadr* is in the last ten nights, while others indicate that it is in the odd nights of the last ten, so the first are general and the second more particular, and the particular has to be given priority over the general. Other *ahaadeeth* state that it is in the last seven - and these are restricted by mention of one who is too weak or unable. So there is no confusion, all the *ahaadeeth* agree and are not contradictory.

---

5. Reported by al-Bukhaaree (4/225) and Muslim (no. 1169).

6. Reported by al-Bukhaaree (4/221) and Muslim (no. 1165).

7. See previous note.

8. Reported by al-Bukhaaree (4/232).

In conclusion: The Muslim should seek out *Lailatul-Qadr* in the odd nights of the last ten: the night of the twenty-first,[9] the twenty-third, the twenty-fifth, the twenty-seventh and the twenty-ninth. If he is too weak or unable to seek it out in all the odd nights, then let him seek it out in the odd nights of the last seven: the night of the twenty-fifth, the twenty-seventh and the twenty-ninth. And Allaah knows best.

• How should a Muslim seek *Lailatul-Qadr*?

One who misses this blessed night then he has missed much good for no one misses it except one from whom it is withheld. Therefore it is recommended that the Muslim who is eager to be obedient to Allaah should stand in Prayer during this night out of *Eemaan* and hoping for the great reward, since if he does this, Allaah will forgive his previous sins.

He (ﷺ) said: *"Whoever stands (in Prayer) in Lailatul-Qadr out of Eemaan and seeking reward then his previous sins are forgiven."*[10]

It is recommended to supplicate a great deal in it, it is reported from 'Aa'ishah, *radiyallahu 'anhaa*, that she said: *"O Messenger of Allaah! What if I knew which night Lailatul-Qadr was, then what should I say in it?"* He said: *"Say:*

اللّٰهُمَّ إِنَّكَ عَفُوٌّ تُحِبُّ الْعَفْوَ فَاعْفُ عَنِّي

(Allaahumma innaka 'affuwwun tuhibbul 'afwa fa'fu 'annee.)
"O Allaah you are the one who pardons greatly, and loves to pardon, so pardon me."[11]

---

9. **Translator's note:** The reader must remember that the night precedes the day. So the twenty-first night is the night before the twenty-first day.

10. Reported by al-Bukhaaree (4/217) and Muslim (no. 759) from Aboo Hurairah.

11. Reported by at-Tirmidhee (no. 3760) and Ibn Maajah (no. 3850). Its *isnaad* is *saheeh*, and for its explanation see *Bughyatul-Ihsaan Fee Wazaa'if Ramadaan* (p. 55-57) of Ibn Rajab al-Hanbalee.

O brother! You know the importance of this night, so stand in Prayer in the last ten nights, in worship, detaching oneself from the women, ordering your family with this, and increasing in actions of obedience and worship in it.

From 'Aa'ishah, *radiyallaahu 'anhaa*, who said: *"The Prophet (ﷺ) used to tighten his waist-wrapper (izaar),*[12] *spend the night in worship, and wake his family in the last ten nights."*[13]

From 'Aa'ishah, *radiyallaahu 'anhaa*: *"Allaah's Messenger (ﷺ)used to exert himself in the last ten nights more than he would at other times."*[14]

• Its signs[15]

Allaah's Messenger (ﷺ) described the morning after *Lailatul-Qadr*, so that the Muslim may know which day it is. From Ubayy, *radiyallaahu 'anhu*, who said: that he (ﷺ) said: *"On the morning following Lailatul-Qadr the sun rises not having any rays, as if it were a brass dish, until it rises up."*[16]

From Aboo Hurairah, *radiyallaahu 'anhu*, who said: *"We were discussing Lailatul-Qadr in the presence of Allaah's Messenger (ﷺ), so he said: 'Which of you remembers [the night] when the moon arose and was like half a plate?'"*[17]

---

12. Meaning he detached himself from his wives in order to worship, and exerted himself in seeking *Lailatul-Qadr*.

13. Reported by al-Bukhaaree (4/233) and Muslim (no. 1174).

14. Reported by Muslim (no. 1174).

15. Many people believe in all sorts of superstitions about *Lailatul-Qadr*, and false beliefs, from them are that trees prostrate, and buildings sleep! and these things are clearly futile and baseless.

16. Reported by Muslim (no. 762), Aboo Daawood, at-Tirmidhee and Ibn Maajah.

17. Reported by Muslim (no. 1170). Qaadee 'Iyaad said: "It contains an indication that it was towards the end of the month - since the moon does not appear like that when it arises except towards the end of the month."

From Ibn 'Abbaas, *radiyallaahu 'anhumaa*, who said: Allaah's Messenger (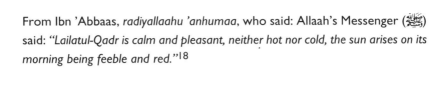)
said: *"Lailatul-Qadr is calm and pleasant, neither hot nor cold, the sun arises on its
morning being feeble and red."*[18]

---

18 Reported by at-Tayaalisee (no. 349), Ibn Khuzaimah (3/231) and al-Bazzaar (1/486). Its *isnaad*
is *hasan*.

Chapter 20

I'tikaaf

• Its wisdom

Ibn al-Qayyim said: "Since the hearts' rectitude and firmness upon the path towards Allaah the Most High, rests upon directing it solely upon Allaah and causing it to turn and give all its attention to Allaah the Most High. Since the disorder of the heart cannot be rectified except by turning to Allaah the Most High, and its disorder will be increased by eating and drinking too much, mixing with the people excessively, speaking profusely and sleeping too much. These will cause it to wander into every valley, and cut it off from its path to Allaah, weaken it, divert it or put a halt to it.

From the Mercy of the Mighty and Most Merciful is that He has prescribed for them fasting, which will cut off the excesses of eating and drinking, and empties the heart of its desires which divert it on its journey to Allaah the Most High. He prescribed it in due proportion as will be appropriate and will benefit the servant, with regard to this world and the Hereafter, and does not harm him, nor damage what is beneficial for him.

He also prescribed *i'tikaaf* for them, by which is intended that the heart is fully occupied with Allaah, the Most High, concentrated upon Him alone, and cut off from preoccupation with the creation. Rather it is engrossed with Him alone, the One free of all defects, such that remembering Him, loving Him and turning to Him takes the place of all anxieties of the heart and its suggestions, such that he is able to overcome them. Thus all his concerns are for Him. His thoughts are all of remembrance of Him, and thinking of how to attain His Pleasure and what will cause nearness to Him. This leads him to feel contented with Allaah instead of the people, so that prepares him for being at peace with Him alone on the day of loneliness in the grave, when there is no one else to give comfort, nor anyone to grant solace except Him. So this is the greater goal of i'tikaaf." [1]

• Its meaning

It means to fully attach oneself to something, so it is used to describe one who habituates the mosque and worships in it. [2]

• Its prescription

It is recommended in Ramadaan and in other days of the year, since it is established that the Prophet (ﷺ) made i'tikaaf for ten days in (the month of) Shawaal. [3]

Also, 'Umar said to the Prophet (ﷺ): "O Messenger of Allaah, I made a vow in the days of Ignorance that I would perform i'tikaaf for a night in the Sacred Mosque (al-Masjidul-Haraam)?" He said: "Then fulfil your vow [and perform i'tikaaf for a night]." [4]

However it is most virtuous in Ramadaan due to the hadeeth of Aboo Hurairah, radiyallaahu 'anhu: "Allaah's Messenger (ﷺ) used to perform i'tikaaf for ten days every Ramadaan, then when it was the year in which he was taken, he

---

1. *Zaadul-Ma'aad* (2/86-87).

2. *Al-Misbaahul-Muneer* (2/424) of al-Fayyoomee and *Lisaanul-'Arab* (9/252) of Ibn Mandhoor.

3. Reported by al-Bukhaaree (4/226) and Muslim (no. 1173).

4. Reported by al-Bukhaaree (4/237) and Muslim (no. 1656).

performed i'tikaaf for twenty days."[5]

The best time is the end of Ramadaan, since the Prophet (ﷺ): *"Used to perform i'tikaaf in the last ten days of Ramadaan until Allaah the Mighty and Majestic, took him."*[6]

• Its preconditions

(a) It is not prescribed except in a mosque, as Allaah, the Most High, says:

وَلَا تُبَٰشِرُوهُنَّ وَأَنتُمْ عَٰكِفُونَ فِى ٱلْمَسَٰجِدِ

"And do not have sexual relations with them (your wives) while you are in *i'tikaaf* in the mosques."[7]

(b) The mosques mentioned here are not to be taken unrestrictedly since a restriction occurs in the authentic *Sunnah* and it is his (ﷺ) saying: *"There is no i'tikaaf except in the three mosques."*[8]

(c) The *Sunnah* for one who is making *i'tikaaf* is that he should fast as has been reported from 'Aa'ishah, *radiyallaahu 'anhaa.*[9]

---

5. Reported by al-Bukhaaree (4/245).

6. Reported by al-Bukhaaree (4/226) and Muslim (no. 1173) from 'Aa'ishah.

7. Sooratul-Baqarah (2):187.

8. This is an established and authentic *hadeeth,* declared *saheeh* by the *imaams* and scholars. As regards its sources and a discussion of it and a reply to the doubts cast by some folk, then refer to the book: *al-Insaaf Fee Ahkaamil-I'tikaaf* of 'Alee Hasan 'Abdul-Hameed, and for further elucidation see *Juzul-I'tikaaf* of al-Hammaamee. The *hadeeth* is reported by al-Baihaqee in his *Sunan* (4/346) and at-Tahaawee in *Mushkilul-Aathaar* (4/20).

[**Publisher's note:** the three mosques that are referred to in the *hadeeth* are the Masjidul-Haraam (Makkah), Masjidun-Nabawee (Madeenah) and Masjidul Aqsa (Jerusalem).]

9. Reported by 'Abdur-Razzaaq in *al-Musannaf* (no. 8037), and he reports its meaning from both Ibn 'Umar and Ibn 'Abbaas, *radiyallaahu 'anhum* (no. 8033).

• Actions permitted for the one making *i'tikaaf*

(a) It is permissible for him to leave the mosque for a need, and he may lean out of the mosque in order for his head to be washed or his hair combed. 'Aa'ishah, *radiyallaahu 'anhaa,* said: *"Allaah's Messenger (ﷺ) used to lean his head to me when he was (making i'tikaaf) in the mosque (and I was in my room) and I would comb it (and in a narration: wash it) [and the threshold of the door was between me and him] [and I was menstruating] and he would not enter the house except for a [person's] needs, when he was making i'tikaaf."*[10]

(b) It is permissible for one making *i'tikaaf* and for others to make *wudoo* in the mosque due to the saying of a man who used to serve the Prophet (ﷺ): *"The Prophet (ﷺ) made a light wudoo in the mosque."*[11]

(c) He may set up a small tent at the back of the mosque and make *i'tikaaf* in it, since 'Aa'ishah, *radiyallaahu 'anhaa,* used to set up a small tent[12] for the Prophet (ﷺ) when he made *i'tikaaf* and this was as he had ordered.[13]

(d) He may place his bedding or mattress in it due to what Ibn 'Umar, *radiyallaahu 'anhumaa,* reports from the Prophet (ﷺ): *"That when he made i'tikaaf, blankets or a mattress would be placed for him behind the pillar of repentance."*[14]

---

10. Reported by al-Bukhaaree (1/342) and Muslim (no. 297). Also refer to *Mukhtasar Saheehil-Bukhaaree* (no. 167) of our Shaikh al-Albaanee and *Jaami'-ul-Usool* (1/341) of Ibn al-Atheer.

11. Reported by Ahmad (5/364) with a *saheeh isnaad.*

12. In Arabic: *Khibbaa':* a tent of animal hair or wool, resting upon two or three supports.

13. Al-Bukhaaree (4/226) and Muslim (no. 1173).

14. Reported by Ibn Maajah (no. 642 of *az-Zawaa'id*) and al-Baihaqee - as al-Boosairee says, through two chains from 'Eesaa ibn 'Umar, from Naafi' from Ibn 'Umar. Its *isnaad* is *hasan.* As for 'Eesaa Ibn 'Umar - then a group narrate from him and he is declared reliable by Ibn Hibbaan, and adh-Dhahabee said: "Some have declared him reliable."

Translator's note: Shaikh al-Albaanee says in his notes to *Saheeh Ibn Khuzaimah* (no. 2236): "Its *isnaad* is *da'eef* (weak). Nu'aim ibn Hammaad is weak and even accused (i.e. of fabrication) by some..."

• A woman's *i'tikaaf*, and her visiting her husband in the mosque

(a) It is permissible for a woman to visit her husband who is making *i'tikaaf*, and he may go with her to the door of the mosque. Safiyyah, *radiyallaahu 'anhaa*, said: The Prophet (ﷺ) *was making i'tikaaf [in the last ten nights of Ramadaan], so I came to visit him at night [and his wives were with him and then departed]. I talked with him for a while, then I stood up to leave, [so he said: "Do not hurry for I will accompany you." He stood along with me to accompany me back - and her dwelling was in the house of Usaamah ibn Zayd [until when he came to the door of the mosque near the door of Umm Salamah], two men of the Ansaar were passing by, when they saw the Prophet (ﷺ) they hastened by, so the Prophet (ﷺ) said: "Be at your ease for she is Safiyyah bint Huyayy." So they said: "Allaah is free from all imperfections! O Messenger of Allaah!" He said: "Indeed Shaitaan circulates in the son of Aadam just as blood circulates, and I feared that he would insert an evil thought" - or he said: "something - into your hearts."*[15]

(b) It is permissible for a woman to make *i'tikaaf* along with her husband or alone as 'Aa'ishah, *radiyallaahu 'anhaa*, said: *"The Prophet (ﷺ) used to perform i'tikaaf in the last ten nights of Ramadaan until Allaah took him, then his wives performed i'tikaaf after him."*[16]

Our Shaikh [al-Albaanee], *hafidhahullaah*, says: "It contains a proof of the permissibility of the *i'tikaaf* of women, and there is no doubt that it is conditional upon the permission of their guardians, and that there is safety from mischief, and from being alone with men - due to the many proofs (forbidding) that, and the *fiqh* principle here is that preventing corruption takes precedence over generating good."

---

15. Reported by al-Bukhaaree (4/240), and Muslim (no. 2157). The final addition is reported by Aboo Daawood (7/142-143).

16. Al-Bukhaaree and Muslim - as has preceded.

Chapter 21

Taraaweeh Prayers

• Its prescription

Taraaweeh[1] prayers in congregation are prescribed as shown by the *hadeeth* of 'Aa'ishah, *radiyallaahu 'anhaa: That Allaah's Messenger (ﷺ) went out in the middle of the night and prayed in the mosque, and the people prayed behind him, then in the morning the people spoke about it. Then a larger number gathered (the second night), and he prayed and they prayed behind him, then the people spoke about it in the morning. On the third night the mosque was crowded, so Allaah's Messenger (ﷺ) came out and the people prayed behind him. Then on the fourth night the mosque could not accommodate the number of people, but he only came out for the morning prayer (salaatus-subh). Then when he finished the morning prayer he turned to the people, repeated the shahaadah and said: "Indeed your presence was not hidden from me, but I feared that it would be made obligatory upon you and that you would not be able to manage it." So Allaah's Messenger (ﷺ) passed away and the situation remained like that."*[2]

When Allaah's Messenger (ﷺ) was taken by his Lord the *Sharee'ah* had been completed and this fear had thus ceased, and so it remained prescribed in congregation - since the reason preventing it had ceased.

---

1. The prayer performed during the nights of Ramadaan.

2. Reported by al-Bukhaaree (3/220) and Muslim (no. 761).

93

This *Sunnah* was revived by the rightly guided Caliph 'Umar ibn al-Khattaab as is mentioned by 'Abdur-Rahmaan ibn 'Abdin al-Qaaree who said: *I went out along with 'Umar ibn al-Khattaab, radiyallaahu 'anhu, in Ramadaan to the mosque and found the people praying in separate groups - a man praying alone or a man leading a small group. So 'Umar said: "I think it would be better if I gathered them all behind a single reciter." Then he made up his mind and gathered them behind Ubayy ibn Ka'b. Then I went out with him on another night and the people were praying behind their reciter, so 'Umar said: "What an excellent innovation this is,[3] and prayer at the time when they sleep is better than at the time when they are praying it." Since the people used to pray in the early part of the night.[4]*

• The number of *rak'ahs*

The people differ about how many *rak'ahs* are to be prayed, and the saying which agrees with the guidance of Muhammad (ﷺ) is that it comprised of eight *rak'ahs* not including the *witr* - as shown by the *hadeeth* of 'Aa'ishah, *radiyallaahu 'anhaa*: *"Allaah's Messenger(ﷺ) did not increase upon eleven rak'ahs in Ramadaan, or outside it."[5]*

The statement of 'Aa'ishah, *radiyallaahu 'anhaa*, is confirmed by Jaabir ibn 'Abdillaah, *radiyallaahu 'anhu*, who mentioned: *"When the Prophet (ﷺ) led the people in prayer, during the night in Ramadaan, he prayed eight rak'ahs and the witr."[6]*

---

3. For a full explanation of the saying of 'Umar: "What an excellent innovation this is..." and that it is not a condonement of innovation in the *Deen* as some people think, refer to *Iqtidaa-us-Siraatil-Mustaqeem* (pp. 275-277) of Ibn Taimiyyah, *al-I'tisaam* of ash-Shaatibee (1/193-195) and *Salaatut-Taraaweeh* of Shaikh al-Albaanee (pp.52-54).

4. Reported by al-Bukhaaree (4/218), Maalik (1/114) and 'Abdur-Razzaaq (no. 7723).

5. Reported by al-Bukhaaree (3/16) and Muslim (no. 736). Al-Haafidh (Ibn Hajr), *rahimahullaah*, says in *al-Fath* (4/54): "And she knew about the Prophet's (ﷺ) practice at night better than anyone else."

6. Reported by Ibn Hibbaan in his *Saheeh* (no. 920), at-Tabaraanee in *as-Sagheer* (p. 108) and Ibn Nasr in *Qiyaamul-Lail* (p. 90). Its *isnaad* is *hasan* as a witness.

When 'Umar ibn al-Khattaab, *radiyallaahu 'anhu*, revived this *Sunnah* he ordered it as eleven *rak'ahs*, in agreement with the authentic *Sunnah*. This is reported by Maalik (1/115) with a *saheeh isnaad*, by way of Muhammad ibn Yoosuf: from as-Saa'ib ibn Yazeed who said: '*Umar ibn al-Khattaab ordered Ubayy ibn Ka'b and Tameem ad-Daaree to lead the people in eleven rak'ahs of prayer, and the reciter would recite soorahs containing hundreds of Aayaat to the extent that we would have to support ourselves due to the length of the standing and we would not depart until the first signs of dawn.*

This narration is contradicted by that of Yazeed ibn Khusaifah who said: "...*with twenty rak'ahs...*" but this narration is *shaadh*.[7]

It cannot be said that it is an addition made by a reliable narrator and therefore acceptable, since a reliable narrators addition cannot contain contradiction. Rather it contains only extra knowledge not found in the narration of the first reliable narrator as occurs in *Fathul-Mugheeth* (1/199), *Mahaasinul-Istilaah* (p. 185) and *al-Kifaayah* (pp. 424-425). Even if the narration of Yazeed were authentic it contains the report of an action, whereas the narration of Muhammad ibn Yoosuf contains a saying (i.e. 'Umar's order to pray eleven *rak'ahs*). As is well known from the principles of *fiqh*, that sayings are given precedence over actions.

'Abdur-Razzaaq reports in his *Musannaf* (No. 7730) from Daawood ibn Qays and others: from Muhammad ibn Yoosuf: from as-Saa'ib ibn Yazeed: "*That 'Umar gathered the people in Ramadaan behind Ubayy ibn Ka'b, and Tameem ad-Daaree, in twenty-one rak'ahs reciting soorahs composed of hundreds of Aayaat, and they would depart at the first signs of dawn.*"

This report contradicts what Maalik narrates from Muhammed ibn Yoosuf: from as-Saa'ib ibn Yazeed, and the *isnaad* of 'Abdur-Razzaaq appears authentic since all its narrators are reliable. Some people attempt to use this narration to claim that the hadeeth of Muhammad ibn Yoosuf is self contradictory

---

7. **Translator's note:** *Shaadh*: Contradicting that which is better established.

(*mudtarab*) - in order to abandon it and prefer the saying that it should be twenty *rak'ahs* as occurs in the *hadeeth* of Yazeed ibn Khusaifah.

This claim is rebutted by the fact that a self-contradictory (*mudtarab*) *hadeeth* is one which is reported more than once from a single narrator, or from two or more narrators, which disagree and are all of similar strength - such that one cannot be preferred to the others.[8]

This condition is not present in the *hadeeth* of Muhammad ibn Yoosuf, since the narration of Maalik can certainly be preferred over that of 'Abdur-Razzaaq on the basis of strength of memory, and we say this taking it to be that the *isnaad* is free from hidden defects. However, this is not case:

(a) There are a number of people who narrate the *Musannaf* from 'Abdur-Razzaaq, one of them is Ishaaq ibn Ibraheem ibn 'Abbaad ad-Dabaree.

(b) This *hadeeth* is one of those narrated by ad-Dabaree from 'Abdul-Razzaaq, since it is he who narrated the *Book of Fasting*.[9]

(c) Ad-Dabaree heard 'Abdur-Razzaaq's works from him at the age of seven.[10]

(d) Ad-Dabaree was not a companion of *hadeeth* and it was not his field.

(e) Therefore he makes many mistakes in what he narrates from 'Abdur-Razzaaq and he reports reprehensible narrations from him which contradict what is authentic. Some scholars have written a whole book containing the mistakes and errors in transmission of ad-Dabaree with regards to the *Musannaf*.[11]

---

8. *Tadreebur-Raawee* (1/262).

9. *Al-Musannaf* (4/153).

10. *Meezaanul-I'tidaal* (1/181).

11. *Meezaanul-I'tidaal* (1/181).

So from what has preceded it can be seen that this is *munkar*[12] since ad-Dabaree contradicts those more reliable than himself. This is one of his errors in transmission - which he has changed from eleven *rak'ahs* to twenty one *rak'ahs* - and you are now aware that his errors are many.[13]

So this narration is *munkar* and a mistake in transmission so it cannot be used as proof. Instead the authentic *Sunnah* reported in *al-Muwatta* (1/115) with an authentic *isnaad* from Muhammad ibn Yoosuf: from as-Saaib ibn Yazeed is established, so be aware.[14]

---

12. **Translator's note:** *Munkar:* that narration which is not only weak, but also contradicts that which is authentic. Also see Glossary.

13. See *Tahdheebut-Tahdheeb* (6/310) and *Meezaanul-I'tidaal* (1/181).

14. For a further discussion and a reply to doubts refer to:
(a) *Al-Kashfus-Sareeh 'An Aghlaatis-Saaboonee Fee Salaatit-Taraaweeh,* of 'Alee Hasan 'Abdul-Hameed.
(b) *Al-Masaabeeh Fee Salaatit-Taraaweeh* of as-Suyootee, with my footnotes.

Chapter 22

Zakaatul-Fitr

• Its ruling

Zakaatul-Fitr is obligatory (*fard*) as shown by the *hadeeth* of Ibn 'Umar, *radiyallaahu 'anhumaa*: *"Allaah's Messenger (ﷺ) obligated Zakaatul-Fitr [for Ramadaan upon the people]"*[1]

And the *hadeeth* of Ibn 'Abbaas, *radiyallaahu 'anhumaa*: *"Allaah's Messenger (ﷺ) obligated Zakaatul-Fitr."*[2]

However some scholars claim that it is abrogated due to the *hadeeth* of Qays ibn Sa'd Ibn 'Ubaadah who said: *"Allaah's Messenger (ﷺ) ordered us to give Sadaqatul-Fitr before Zakaah was made obligatory, so when Zakaah was made obligatory he neither ordered us nor forbade us, and we practice it."*

Al-Haafidh Ibn Hajr, *rahimahullaah*, replies to this *hadeeth*, saying (3/368): "Its *isnaad* contains an unknown narrator,[3] and that even if it were authentic then it is not a proof of abrogation since perhaps the original order was sufficient,

---

1. Reported by al-Bukhaaree (3/291) and Muslim (no. 984) the addition is his.

2. Reported by Aboo Daawood (no. 1622) and an-Nasaa'ee (5/50). Its chain of narrations contains the *'an'anah* of al-Hasan, but it is witnessed to by the previous narration.

3. However he is supported in this narration, since it is reported by an-Nasaa'ee (5/49), Ibn Maajah (1/585), Ahmad (6/6), Ibn Khuzaimah (4/81), al-Haakim (1/410) and al-Baihaqee (4/159) through various *isnaads*. Its chain of narration is *saheeh*.

since the revelation of one obligation does not mean the removal of another obligation."

Al-Khattaabee says in *Ma'aalimus-Sunan* (2/214): "This does not show that its obligation has ceased, since the increase of a certain type of worship does not necessarily mean abrogation of the original action of worship which has been added to, except that both Zakaah of wealth and *Zakaatul-Fitr* are given to the poor."

• **Whom is it obligatory upon?**

It is obligatory upon every Muslim, the young and the old, the male and the female, and the free and the slave, due to the *hadeeth* of 'Abdullaah ibn 'Umar, *radiyallaahu 'anhumaa*: "Allaah's Messenger (ﷺ) made Zakaatul-Fitr of a saa'[4] of dates, or a saa' of barley, obligatory upon the slave and the free, the male and the female, and the young and the old of the Muslims."[5]

Some scholars hold it to be obligatory upon the infidel (*kaafir*) slave as well due to the *hadeeth* of Aboo Hurairah, *radiyallaahu 'anhu*: "No charity is binding upon the slave except Sadaqatul-Fitr."[6]

However this *hadeeth* is general whereas the *hadeeth* of Ibn 'Umar is more particular, and as is known the particular takes precedence over the general. Others say: It is only obligatory upon one who fasted due to the *hadeeth* of Ibn 'Abbaas: "Allaah's Messenger (ﷺ) obligated Zakaatul-Fitr as a purification for the fasting person from loose talk and indecent speech, and to feed the poor."[7]

---

4. See Glossary.

5. Reported by al-Bukhaaree (3/291) and Muslim (no. 984).

6. Reported by Muslim (no. 982).

7. Reported by Aboo Daawood (no. 1622)], an-Nasaa'ee (5/49, 5/50), Ibn Maajah (1/585) and others. The *hadeeth* is *hasan*.

Al-Khattaabee, *rahimahullaah,* says in *Ma'aalimus-Sunan* (2/214): "It is obliga-tory upon every wealthy fasting person or poor person who has in excess of his need, since its obligation is in order to purify - and all of those fasting need this. So if they are all the same in their need for it (i.e. purification), then they are all the same as regards its obligation."

Al-Haafidh, *rahimahullaah,* replies (3/369) saying: "The fact that purification is mentioned, then this is a general statement, not meaning that it is not obligatory upon one who has not committed these sins or such a one whose piety is assured, or one who accepts Islaam a moment before the sun sets (on the final day of fasting)."

Some of them hold it to be an obligation which has to be carried out on behalf of the unborn child, however we do not know of any proof for this - nor is he described as a *young one* in the language or in practice.

• What is acceptable as *zakaatul-fitr*

Zakaatul-Fitr may be given in the form of a *saa'* of barley, or a *saa'* of dates, or a *saa'* of dried curds, or a *saa'* of raisins, or rye, due to the *hadeeth* of Aboo Sa'eed al-Khudree, *radiyallaahu 'anhu:* "*We used to give Zakaatul-Fitr as a saa' of grain (ta'aam) or a saa' of barley, or a saa' of dates, or a saa' of dried curds, or a saa' of raisins.*"[8]

The *hadeeth* of Ibn 'Umar, *radiyallaahu 'anhumaa,* who said: He (ﷺ) said: "*Sadaqatul-Fitr was made obligatory as a saa' of barley, or a saa' of dates, or a saa' of rye.*"[9]

The people of knowledge have differed about the meaning of *ta'aam* in the *hadeeth* of Aboo Sa'eed, *radiyallaahu 'anhu.* It is explained to mean: wheat, and

---

8. Reported by al-Bukhaaree (3/294) and Muslim (no. 985).

9. Reported by Ibn Khuzaimah (4/80) and al-Haakim (1/408-410).

it is said: other than this. What one feels satisfied with is that it is general covering all kinds of grain such as wheat and the other types just mentioned, also flour and (barley) gruel. All of this was done in the time of Allaah's Messenger (ﷺ) as shown by the *hadeeth* of Ibn 'Abbaas, *radiyallaahu 'anhumaa*, who said: *"Allaah's Messenger (ﷺ) ordered us to give the zakaah of Ramadaan as a saa' of grain for the young and the old, the free and the slave. Whoever gave rye - then it will be accepted from him and I think that he said: He who gives flour it will be accepted from him, and he who gives (barley) gruel it will be accepted."*[10]

From Ibn 'Abbaas, *radiyallaahu 'anhu*, that he used to say: *"He who brings wheat it will be accepted from him, whoever brings barley it will be accepted from him, whoever brings dates it will be accepted from him, whoever brings rye it will be accepted from him, and whoever brings raisins it will be accepted from him, and I think he said: Whoever brings (barley) gruel it will be accepted from him."*[11]

As regards the *ahaadeeth* which deny the presence of wheat, or the fact that Mu'aawiyah, *radiyallaahu anhu*, held that half a *saa'* of brownish wheat of Shaam[12] should be given and that it is equivalent to a full *saa'* - then it should be taken to refer to the fact that these types were rare, whereas the others mentioned were their common food stuffs and this is supported by the saying of Aboo Sa'eed: *"And our food was barley, raisins, dried curds and dates."*[13]

The argument of those who disagree is lost by what follows as regards the explanation of its quantity in the clear and authentic *ahaadeeth* containing mention of wheat, that two *mudd's*[14] of it are equivalent to a *saa'*. So the

---

10. Reported by Ibn Khuzaimah (4/80) with a *saheeh isnaad*.

11. Reported by Ibn Khuzaimah (4/80) with a *saheeh isnaad*.

12. **Publisher's note:** The area that contains present day Syria and Jordon.

13. Al-Bukhaaree and Muslim.

14. See Glossary.

Muslim gives due respect to the Companions of Allaah's Messenger (ﷺ) and realises that Mu'aawiyah was not making his own *ijtihaad*, but rather his proof was the *hadeeth* of the truthful and trustworthy Messenger (ﷺ).

• Its quantity

The Muslim should give one *saa'* of the aforementioned types of food stuffs. There is difference regarding wheat, so some say: half a *saa'* of it should be given, and it is what is correct due to his (ﷺ) saying: *"Give a saa' of wheat or wheat-grain for two people; or a saa' of dates, or a saa' of barley for every free person and slave, and young and old."*[15]

The *saa'* referred to here is the *saa'* of the people of al-Madeenah as shown by the *hadeeth* of Ibn 'Umar, *radiyallaahu 'anhumaa*: *"Weighing is according to the weights of the people of Makkah, and measures are according to the measure of the people of al-Madeenah."*[16]

• On whose behalf should a man give it?

The Muslim gives it for himself and for those whom he takes care of: young or old, male or female, free or slave - due to the *hadeeth* of Ibn 'Umar, *radiyallaahu 'anhumaa*: *"Allaah's Messenger ordered Sadaqatul-Fitr on behalf of the young and the old, and the free and the slave - whom you provide for."*[17]

---

15. Reported by Ahmad (5/432) from Tha'labah ibn Su'air. Its narrators are all reliable, and it has a witnessing narration reported by ad-Daaraqutnee (2/151) from Jaabir with a *saheeh isnaad*.

16 Reported by Aboo Daawood (no. 2340), an-Nasaa'ee (7/281), and al-Baihaqee (6/31) from Ibn 'Umar with a *saheeh isnaad*.

17. Reported by ad-Daaraqutnee (2/141) and al-Baihaqee (4/161) from Ibn 'Umar with a weak *isnaad*. It is reported by al-Baihaqee (4/161) through a different chain which is broken, from 'Alee. It is reported through another chain as the saying of Ibn 'Umar by Ibn Abee Shaibah in *al-Musannaf* (4/37) with a *saheeh isnaad*. So it is *hasan* due to their chains.

• To whom should it be given?

It may not be given except to those who have the right to it, and they are the poor as occurs in the *hadeeth* of Ibn 'Abbaas, *radiyallaahu 'anhumaa*: *"Allaah's Messenger (ﷺ) obligated Zakaatul-Fitr as purification for the fasting person from loose talk and indecent speech, and to feed to poor."*[18]

This is the view preferred by Shaikhul-Islaam Ibn Taimiyyah in *Majmoo' ul-Fataawaa* (25/71-78) and his student Ibnul-Qayyim in his valuable book *Zaadul-Ma'aad* (2/44). There are some scholars who hold that it can be given to all the eight categories who can receive zakaah - but this has no proof and Shaikhul-Islaam replies to this in the aforementioned work, so refer to it for it is important.

It is from the *Sunnah* that there should be a person with whom it is gathered just as the Prophet (ﷺ) entrusted Aboo Hurairah, *radiyallaahu 'anhu*, who said: *"Allaah's Messenger (ﷺ) entrusted me to look after the zakaah of Ramadaan."*[19]

Ibn 'Umar, *radiyallaahu 'anhu*, used to give some of it to those who would accept it - and they were those whom the *imaam* sent to collect it, and that was a day or two before *Eidul-Fitr*. It is reported by Ibn Khuzaimah (4/83) by way of 'Abdul-Waarith from Ayyoob: *I said: "When did Ibn 'Umar used to give the saa'?" He said: "When the collectors had finished." I said: "When did the collectors finish?" He said: "A day or two days before the day of Fitr."*

---

18. Reported by Aboo Daawood, an-Nasaa'ee and Ibn Maajah. The *hadeeth* is *hasan*.

19. Reported by al-Bukhaaree (4/396).

• When is it to be given

It is to be given before the people go out for the 'Eid prayer.[20] It is not permissible to delay it until after the prayer, nor to give it in advance, except by a day or two. As is reported from the practice of Ibn 'Umar, *radiyallaahu 'anhu*, since the narrator of a *hadeeth* will be the one who best knows its meaning. If it is delayed until after the prayer then it will count only as charity, due to the *hadeeth* of Ibn 'Abbaas, *radiyallahu 'anhumaa*: *"...and whoever gives it after the prayer, then it is merely a sadaqah."*[21]

• Its wisdom

It has been prescribed by the Wise Legislator as a purification for those who fasted, from loose and indecent talk, and to feed the poor Muslims so that they have enough provision for that day - as is shown by the previous *hadeeth* of Ibn 'Abbaas, *radiyallaahu 'anhumaa*.

---

20. See *Salaatul-'Eidain Fis-Sunnatil-Mutahharah* of Shaikh 'Alee Hasan 'Abdul-Hameed.

21. Reported by Aboo Daawood, an-Nasaa'ee and Ibn Maajah as has preceded. It is *hasan*.

Chapter 23

Some Oft-Quoted Weak *Ahaadeeth*

We decided to add this chapter to the book due to its obvious importance, and as a warning to the people and a clear statement of the truth, so we say:

Allaah, the One free of all imperfections and Most High, has appointed for the *Sunnah* of the Prophet (ﷺ) trustworthy bearers who expel from it the alterations of the people of falsehood, the misinterpretations of those going beyond bounds, and uncovering the false accretions added to it by those who try to adulterate it.

Throughout the ages many accretions have been mixed with it, either weak *ahaadeeth*, lies or fabrications and the like and this has been fully explained and made clear by the scholars throughout the ages. One who looks today into the works of writers and speeches of admonition will see that they do not give the slightest attention to this matter except those upon whom is Allaah's Mercy, even though scholarly reference works, which explain which *ahaadeeth* are authentic and uncover the weak narrations, are readily available.

In explaining this matter and its evil consequences upon the knowledge and the people, we do not intend to rebuke or accuse anyone. We will just quote some examples of narrations which have been introduced and become well known amongst the people, to the point that you will hardly read an article or hear an admonition except that the weak *ahaadeeth* have a prominent place in it.

So acting upon his (ﷺ) saying: *"Convey from me even if it is only a single Aayah..."*[1]

And his (ﷺ) saying: *"The Deen is sincerity and sincere advising..."*[2]

So we say: The weak *ahaadeeth* which have become widespread amongst the people, at every level, are very many, to the point that very few manage to mention anything authentic - despite its being plentiful also. May Allaah have mercy upon the Imaam 'Abdullaah Ibn al-Mubaarak who said: *"There is sufficiency in the authentic ahaadeeth so there is no need for what is weak."* So let this *imaam* be our example, and let us stick to the authentic and pure knowledge.

From the weak *ahaadeeth* which people commonly quote concerning Ramadaan are:

1. "If the servants knew how great Ramadaan was, then they would wish that Ramadaan lasted all year. Indeed Paradise is decorated for Ramadaan from the start of the year till the next year..." and it is a long *hadeeth*.

This *hadeeth* is reported by Ibn Khuzaimah (No. 1886), Ibn al-Jawzee in *Kitaabul-Mawdoo'aat* (2/188-189) and Aboo Ya'laa in his *Musnad* as occurs in *al-Mataalibul-'Aaliyah* (46/a-b manuscript) by way of Jareer ibn Ayyoob al-Bajalee: from ash-Sha'bee: from Naafi' ibn Burdah: from Aboo Mas'ood al-Ghifaaree.

This *hadeeth* is fabricated (*mawdoo'*), the cause being Jareer ibn Ayyoob. Ibn Hajr quotes his biography in *Lisaanul-Meezaan* (2/101) and says: *"Famous for his weakness."* Then he quotes the saying of Aboo Nu'aim about him: *"He used to fabricate ahaadeeth,"* from al-Bukhaaree: *"Munkar in narrating hadeeth,"* and from an-Nasaa'ee: *"Abandoned!"*

---

1. Reported by al-Bukhaaree (6/361).

2. Reported by Muslim (no. 55).

Ibn al-Jawzee declared it to be fabricated, and Ibn Khuzaimah said after relating it: *"If the narration is authentic, since there is some doubt in the heart about Jareer Ibn Ayyoob al-Bajalee."*

2. "O people a very great month has come upon you, a month containing a night better than a thousand months. Allaah has made it an obligation to fast in it, and standing in prayer in its night is a superogatory action. Whoever seeks nearness to Him with a good deed in it will be like one performing an obligatory action in other months... It is a month the beginning of which is a mercy, the middle is forgiveness, and its end is a granting of freedom from the Fire..."
It is also a long *hadeeth* and we have quoted the most well-known parts of it.

This *hadeeth* is also reported by Ibn Khuzaimah (No. 1887), al-Mahaamulee in his *Amaalee* (No. 293), and al-Asbahaanee in *at-Targheeb* (Q/178, B-manuscript) by way of 'Alee ibn Zayd ibn Jud'aan: from Sa'eed ibn al-Musaayib: from Salmaan.

This *isnaad* is *da'eef* due to the weakness of 'Alee ibn Zayd. Ibn Sa'd says about him, *"He is somewhat weak, he is not used as a proof."* Ahmad ibn Hanbal said: *"He is not strong."* Ibn Ma'een said: *"He is weak."* Ibn Abee Khaithumah said: *"Weak in everything."* Ibn Khuzaimah said: *"I do not accept him as a proof due to his weak memory."* - as occurs in *at-Tahdheeb* (7/322-323).

Ibn Khuzaimah said after quoting his narration: *"If the narration is authentic."* Ibn Hajr says in *al-Atraaf*: *"It is narrated by 'Alee ibn Zayd ibn Jud'aan alone and he is weak"* as As-Suyootee quotes from him in *Jam'ul-Jawaami'* (No. 24,714). Ibn Abee Haatim reports from his father in *'Ilalul-Hadeeth* (1/249) that he said: *"The hadeeth is munkar!"*

3. "Fast and you will be healthy."

It is part of a *hadeeth* reported by Ibn 'Adiyy in *al-Kaamil* (7/2521) by way of Nahshal ibn Sa'eed: from ad-Dahhaak: from Ibn 'Abbaas. At-Tabaraanee reports it in *al-Awsat* (1/Q, 69 A-manuscript of *Majma' ul-Bahrain*) and Aboo Nu'aim in *at-Tibbun-Nabawee* as occurs in *Takhreejul-Ihyaa'* (7/401) by way of Muhammad ibn Sulaimaan ibn Abee Daawood: from Zuhair ibn Muhammad: Suhail Ibn Abee Saalih: from Aboo Hurairah.

Its *isnaad* is weak. Aboo Bakr al-Athrum said: *"I heard Ahmad say - and he mentioned the narration of the people of Shaam from Zuhair ibn Muhammad, he said: 'They report ahaadeeth from him which are munkar.'"*

Aboo Haatim said: *"There is some weakness in his memory, his ahaadeeth narrated in Iraaq are better than his hadeeth narrated in Shaam due to his weak memory."* Al-'Ijlee said: *"These ahaadeeth which the people of Shaam narrate from him do not please me,"* as occurs in *Tahdheebul-Kamaal* (9/417).

Muhammad Ibn Sulaimaan is from Shaam and has a biography in *Taareekh Dimishq* (15 Q,386 - manuscript) - so his narrations from Zuhair, as the scholars have stated, are *munkar* and this *hadeeth* is one of them!

4. "He who abandons fasting during a day of Ramadaan without a valid excuse, or illness - then even if he were to fast for ever it would not make up for it."

This *hadeeth* is quoted in disconnected form by al-Bukhaaree in his *Saheeh* (*Fathul-Baaree*, 4/160) without an *isnaad*. It is connected by Ibn Khuzaimah in his *Saheeh* (No. 1987), at-Tirmidhee (No. 723) Aboo Daawood (No. 2397), Ibn Maajah (No. 1672), an-Nasaa'ee in *al-Kubraa* as occurs in *Tuhfatul Ashraaf* (10/373), al-Baihaqee (4/228) and Ibn Hajr in *Taghleequt-Ta'leeq* (3/170) by way of Abul-Mutawwas: from his father: from Aboo Hurairah.

Ibn Hajr says in *Fathul-Baaree* (4/161): *"They disagree greatly in their narration from Habeeb ibn Abee Thaabit, it has three weaknesses: (i) contradiction of its narrators, (ii) the condition of Abul-Mutawwas is unknown, (iii) doubt about whether his father met Aboo Hurairah or not."*

Ibn Khuzaimah says after reporting it: *"If the narration is authentic, since I do not know Abul-Mutawwas or his father."* So this *hadeeth* is also weak.

These are four *ahaadeeth* which have been declared weak and unreliable by the scholars, yet we still hear them and see them every day in the blessed month of Ramadaan in particular, and at other times. It is apparent that some of these *ahaadeeth* contain parts whose meaning is correct and established in our *Sharee'ah* in the Book or the *Sunnah*. However this on its own does not allow us to attribute to Allaah's Messenger (ﷺ) that which is not established authentically from him, particularly since this *Ummah* alone - to the exception of all previous nations has been particularised by Allaah, the One free of all imperfections, with the use of *isnaads* (chains of narration). Through them we can ascertain what is acceptable and what has been invented, and what is authentic *(saheeh)* from that which is not. It is a very precise branch of knowledge, and he indeed spoke well who described it as: *"The study of what is narrated and the measure for the authenticity of narrations."*

Epilogue

O brother keen to act in obedience to Allaah, the Living, the Sustainer of Everything, before you is the description of how the Prophet (ﷺ) fasted - its details are no longer hidden from you, so hasten to the abundant good, cling to that and turn, with the understanding which Allaah has given you, away from sin.

"How perfect and free from all defects You are O Allaah, and all Praise and thanks are for You. I bear witness that none has the right to be worshipped but You. I ask for Your forgiveness and turn in repentance to You."

Written by:

Two students of the knowledge
brought by the Prophet (ﷺ):

Saleem al-Hilaalee and
'Alee Hasan 'Alee 'Abdul-Hameed
25th. Ramadaan 1403 H.

Glossary

'Aalim: scholar.

Aayah (pl. Aayaat): a Sign of Allaah; a verse of the Qur'aan.

Aayaat: See *Aayah*.

'Abd: worshipper

Aboo (Abee, Abaa): father of; used as a means of identification.

'Alaihisalaam: "may Allaah protect and preserve him." It is said after the name of a Prophet of Allaah or after the name of an angel.

Adhaan: the Call to Prayer.

Ahaadeeth: See *Hadeeth*.

'An'anah: a narrator's reporting by saying 'from so and so' not describing exactly in what form it was transmitted to him. This will only affect the authenticity of the narration if the one doing it is a *mudallis*.

Bid'ah: innovation; anything introduced into the *Deen*, in order to seek Allaah's pleasure, not having a specific proof or basis in the *Deen*.

Companions (Ar. *Sahaabah*): the Muslims who saw the Prophet (ﷺ) and died upon Islaam.

Da'eef: weak; unauthentic (narration).

Deen: way of life prescribed by Allaah i.e. Islaam.

Dhikr: remembrance of Allaah with the heart and tongue, and remembrance of what He has ordered and prohibited.

Du'aa: invocation; supplication.

Eemaan: faith; to affirm all that was revealed to the Messenger (ﷺ), affirming with the heart, testifying with the tongue and acting with the limbs. The actions of the limbs are from the completeness of *Eemaan*. Faith increases with obedience to Allaah and decreases with disobedience.

Fiqh: the understanding and application of the *Sharee'ah* from its sources.

Hadeeth (pl. **Ahaadeeth**): narration concerning the utterances of the Prophet (ﷺ), his actions or an attribute of his.

Hafidhahullaah: "may Allaah protect him." Usually said after the name of a scholar who is still alive.

Hajj: pilgrimage to Makkah.

Halaal: permitted under the *Sharee'ah*.

Haraam: prohibited under the *Sharee'ah*.

Hasan: fine; term used for an authentic *hadeeth*, which does not reach the higher category of *Saheeh*.

Hijrah: migration from the unlawful to the lawful or from the lands of the disbelievers to the land of Islaam.

Hukm (pl. **Ahkaam**): ruling; judgement. In the *Sharee'ah* all actions fall into one of five categories:

(1) *Fard/Waajib* (Obligatory): One who does it is rewarded and one who leaves it without an excuse is deserving of punishment.

(2) *Mustahabb/Mandoob* (Recommended): One who does it is rewarded, but one who leaves it is not punished.

(3) *Mubaah* (Permissible/Allowable): There is no reward or punishment for either doing it or leaving it.

(4) *Makrooh* (Disliked/Undesirable): One who avoids it is rewarded but one who does it is not punished.

(5) *Haraam* (Forbidden): One who does it deserves punishment and one who avoids it is rewarded.

'Ibaadah: worship; worship of Allaah.

Ibn: son of; used as a means of identification.

Iftaar: breaking (i.e. ending) the fast.

Ijmaa': consensus; a unified opinion of scholars regarding an issue.

Ijtihaad: exertion of effort; the process of arising at a reasoned decision by a scholar on an issue.

Imaam: leader; leader in *Salaah*, knowledge or *fiqh*; leader of a state.

Isnaad: the chain of narrators linking the collector of the saying to the person quoted.

Kaafir (pl. **Kuffaar**): a rejector of Islaam i.e. a disbeliever.

Marfoo': raised; a narration attributed to the Prophet (ﷺ).

Mawdoo': fabricated; spurious; invented (narration).

Mawqoof: stopped; a narration from a *Companion*.

Mawsool: connected; a continuous *isnaad*.

Mu'allaq: a narration where one or more consecutive narrators are missing from the end of its chain (i.e. where the scholar of *hadeeth* does not quote his immediate authority).

Mudallis: most commonly a narrator who reports things from his Shaikh which he did not directly hear from him but from an intermediate whom he does not name but instead says 'from the Shaikh'. This intermediate may be weak. The scholars of *hadeeth* will only accept the narrations of a *mudallis* when he clearly states that he heard them from the Shaikh, i.e. 'The Shaikh narrated to us..' e.t.c.

Mudd: the amount held by both hands cupped together.

Mudtarab: a narration which has different versions, either in text or chain, which are mutually contradictory and it is not possible to ascertain what is correct.

Muhaddith: scholar of the science of *hadeeth*.

Mujtahid: one who is qualified to pass judgements using *ijtihaad*.

Munkar: rejected; a narration which in itself is not authentic and also contradicts other authentic narrations.

Munqati': a narration with a missing link or links in the chain of narration.

Mursal: loose; a narration in which a *Successor* narrated directly from the Prophet (ﷺ), i.e. omitting the *Companion* from who he heard it.

Radiyallaahu 'anhu/'anhaa/'anhum/'anhumaa: may Allaah be pleased with him/her/them/both of them.

Rahimahullaah/Rahimahumullaah: may Allaah bestow His mercy upon him/them.

Saa': four *mudds*.

Sahaabah: the *Companions* of the Prophet (ﷺ). See *Companions*.

Saheeh: correct; an authentic narration.

Salaf: predecessors; the early Muslims; the Muslims of the first three generations: the *Companions*, the *Successors* and their successors.

Salafee: one who ascribes himself to the *Salaf* and follows in their way.

Shaadh: unusual; a narration whose narrators are reliable but they contradict that which is better established and more authentic.

Sha'baan: the eighth month of the Islamic calendar. It is the month preceding Ramadaan.

Shaikh: scholar.

Sharee'ah: the Divine code of Law.

Shawaal: the tenth month of the Islamic calendar. It is the month after Ramadaan.

Siwaak (Miswaak): a stick which is used to clean the teeth.

Successor (Ar. *Taabi'i* pl. *Taabi'een*): a Muslim (other than another *Companion*) who met a *Companion*.

Suhoor: pre-dawn meal taken before fasting.

Sunnah: in its broadest sense, the entire *Deen* which the Prophet (ﷺ) came with and taught, i.e. all matters of belief, rulings, manners and actions which were conveyed by the *Companions*. It also includes those matters which the Prophet (ﷺ) established by his sayings, actions and tacit approval - as opposed to *bid'ah* (innovation).

sunnah: an action of the Prophet (ﷺ).

Soorah: a chapter of the Qur'aan.

Taqwa: *taqwa* is acting in obedience to Allaah, hoping for His mercy upon light from Him and *Taqwa* is leaving acts of disobedience, out of fear of Him, upon light from Him.

Tawheed: Allaah is the only Lord of creation, He, alone, is their Provider and Sustainer, Allaah has Names and attributes which none of the creation share and Allaah is to be singled out for worship, alone.

Tawheed is maintaining the Oneness of Allaah in all the above mentioned categories. Islaam makes a clear distinction between the Creator and the creation. *Shirk* (associating partners with Allaah) begins when this becomes blurred and the person fails to recognize the difference between Allaah and that which Allaah created. This leads the person to end up worshipping the creation instead of the Creator.